CONCEPTS IN SCIENCE

CURIE EDITION

CONSULTING SPECIALISTS IN THE SCIENCES

LAWRENCE P. EBLIN, *Chemistry*
Professor, Ohio University, Athens, Ohio
GARRETT HARDIN, *Biology and Ecology*
Professor, University of California, Santa Barbara
RICHARD C. LEWONTIN, *Biology and Genetics*
Professor, Harvard University, Cambridge, Massachusetts
ALISTAIR McCRONE, *Geology and Earth Science*
Professor, University of the Pacific, Stockton, California
FRANKLIN MILLER, JR., *Physics*
Chairman of Department, Kenyon College, Gambier, Ohio
FLETCHER G. WATSON, *Astronomy and Science Education*
Professor Emeritus, Harvard University, Cambridge, Massachusetts

THE AUTHORS

PAUL F. BRANDWEIN
Consultant to Schools on Curriculum and Instruction
Adjunct Professor, University of Pittsburgh
ELIZABETH K. COOPER
formerly Director of Elementary Education
Santa Monica, California
PAUL E. BLACKWOOD
Chief, Southeast Program Operations Branch
U.S. Office of Education*
MARGARET COTTOM-WINSLOW
Director of Curriculum, ICEA
New York, New York
JOHN A. BOESCHEN
formerly Science Teacher
Pinole, California
MORSLEY G. GIDDINGS
Professor of Education
Brooklyn College, City University of New York
FRANK ROMERO
Coordinator, Dallas Independent School District
Dallas, Texas
ARTHUR A. CARIN
Professor of Elementary and Early Childhood Education
Queens College, City University of New York

*The work of Paul Blackwood on the *Concepts in Science* Series was done in his private capacity, and no official endorsement by the U.S. Office of Education is intended or should be inferred.

This series is dedicated to Marie Curie, one of the great and noble scientists of the world.

CONCEPTS IN SCIENCE

CURIE EDITION

Paul F. Brandwein
Elizabeth K. Cooper
Paul E. Blackwood
Margaret Cottom-Winslow
John A. Boeschen
Morsley G. Giddings
Frank Romero
Arthur A. Carin

HARCOURT BRACE JOVANOVICH
New York Chicago San Francisco Atlanta Dallas *and* London

COVER: Fran Hall, Photo Researchers.

HALF-TITLE PAGE: S. J. Krasemann, Peter Arnold.

ILLUSTRATORS: David M. Carroll; Eva Cellini; Felix Cooper; Pam Carroll; John Murphy; Howard Friedman; Judy Skorpil; Dick Morrill, Inc.; Cynthia Scull; HBJ art staff.

PHOTOGRAPHERS: Oscar Buitrago, Glyn Cloyd, Eric Maristany, Erik Arnesen, Richard Watherwax, James Theologos, Robin Forbes, Padraic Cooper, George T. Resch.

PICTURE ACKNOWLEDGMENTS

Key: (t) top, (b) bottom, (l) left, (r) right, (c) center.

HBJ PHOTOS Pages 7 (t), 8, 9, 21, 23 (t), 28 (b), 29 (cl), 33, 34, 37, 42, 43, 44, 48, 49, 54, 56 (tl), 59, 60, 61, 62, 63, 65, 66, 67, 70, 71, 72, 73, 74, 75, 76, 79, 80 (t) (b), 81, 82, 83, 84, 85, 86, 91, 93, 96, 97, 98, 99, 100 (bl) (br), 101, 103, 104, 105, 106, 110, 112, 113, 114, 117, 118, 119, 120, 124, 125, 126 (c) (b), 127 (cl) (cr), 138, 139, 142, 147, 157, 160, 170, 171, 172, 173, 174, 175, 176, 178, 179, 181, 182, 183, 184, 186, 187, 188, 189 (bl) (br), 190, 191, 192, 193, 196, 198, 199, 200 (t) (c), 201 (tr), 216, 229 (b).

RESEARCH PHOTOS Pages vi: NASA 2: Dr. E. R. Degginger. 3: D. Wallin, Taurus. 5: (t) F. J. Alsop, Bruce Coleman; (b) S. J. Krasemann, Peter Arnold. 7: (b) John Colwell, Grant Heilman. 19: Ron Austing, Photo Researchers. 23: (b) Runk/Schoenberger, Grant Heilman. 27: (t) Norman Owen Tomalin, Bruce Coleman; (b) Robert Dunne, Photo Researchers. 28: (t) Dr. E. R. Degginger; (c) S. J. Krasemann, Peter Arnold. 29: (tl) Lizabeth Corlett, DPI; (tr) Joe Bilbao, Photo Researchers; (bl) Dr. J. A. L. Cooke, Bruce Coleman; (br) Hal McKusick, DPI. 30–31: Runk/Schoenberger, Grant Heilman. 32: G. R. Roberts. 35: Burnett Cross. 36: Hans Reinhard, Bruce Coleman. 41: Ken Brate, Photo Researchers. 46: Alfred Owczarzak, Taurus. 47: (t) Laurence Pringle, Photo Researchers; (b) Russ Kinne, Photo Researchers. 50: John H. Atkinson, Jr., DPI. 52: (t) L. West, Bruce Coleman; (b) Runk/Schoenberger, Grant Heilman. 53: Jacques Jangoux, Peter Arnold. 55: (t) G. R. Roberts; (c) Hans Reinhard, Bruce Coleman; (b) Laurence Pringle, Photo Researchers. 56: (cl) William R. Wright, Taurus; (bl) Jack Fields, Photo Researchers; (r) Kenneth W. Fink, Bruce Coleman. 57: (l) L. West, Bruce Coleman; (r) Dr. E. R. Degginger. 58: Van Bucher, Photo Researchers. 68: (both) Dr. E. R. Degginger. 69: Herbert Lanks, Monkmeyer. 77–78: Grant Heilman. 80: (c) Herbert Lanks, Monkmeyer, 87: Sequeira, Rapho Guillumette/Photo Researchers. 88: Bruce Roberts, Photo Researchers. 89: W. R. Wilson, FPG. 92: Jack Ryan, National Audubon Society/Photo Researchers. 94: Shostal. 95: (l) Dr. E. R. Degginger; (r) Department of Energy. 100: (t) Russ Kinne, Photo Researchers. 102: Shostal. 107: Charles Colby, Photo Researchers. 108: Grant Heilman. 111: Bucky Reeves, National Audubon Society/Photo Researchers. 116: Felix Cooper. 121: Ray Atkeson. 122: T. W. Putney, Delaware Photo Library. 126: (t) Bruce Roberts, Photo Researchers. 127: (b) Courtesy of National Coal Association. 128–129: NASA. 134: NASA. 137: (l) Thase Daniel, Bruce Coleman; (r) Nicholas deVore III, Bruce Coleman. 143–145: NASA. 148: NASA. 149: Lick Observatory. 150: NASA. 151: (t) NASA; (b) Lick Observatory. 152–153: NASA. 154: Lick Observatory. 155 © California Institute of Technology and Carnegie Institute of Washington, photo from Hale Observatories. 156: NASA. 159: Russ Kinne, Photo Researchers. 161–164: NASA. 165: (t) (c) NASA; (b) Lick Observatory. 168: J. Zimmerman, FPG. 169: David Herman, Taurus. 194: Ewing Galloway. 195: Tom McHugh, Photo Researchers. 197: John Groothoff, Guidance Assoc. 200: (b) Tom McHugh, Photo Researchers. 201: (tl) Bill Brooks, Bruce Coleman. 202: Dr. M. F. Soper, Bruce Coleman. 203: Mario Fantin, Photo Researchers. 204: (t) Jeff Foott, Bruce Coleman; (b) Kenneth W. Fink, Photo Researchers. 205: (t) Jeff Foott, Bruce Coleman; (b) Bruce A. Macdonald, Animals, Animals. 206: (t) J. R. Simon, Bruce Coleman; (b) Peter Simon, Photo Researchers. 207: (tl) Anthony Mercieca, National Audubon Society/Photo Researchers; (tr) (b) Jen & Des Bartlett, Bruce Coleman. 208: (t) Dr. E. R. Degginger; (b) J. H. Carmichael, Bruce Coleman. 209: (t) (b) Hans Reinhard, Bruce Coleman. 210: (tl) George Holton, Photo Researchers; (tr) Grant Heilman; (bl) Zig Leszczynski, Animals, Animals; (br) Lee Foster, Bruce Coleman. 217: Grant Heilman. 219: Karl Kenyon. 220: W. Morgan, National Audubon Society/Photo Researchers. 221: Rapho Guillumette/Photo Researchers. 222: Douglas Faulkner. 223: (t) R. Robert Abrams, Bruce Coleman; (b) Anthony Mercieca, National Audubon Society/Photo Researchers. 224: (tl) Douglas Faulkner; (tr) Lynwood Chace, National Audubon Society/Photo Researchers. 225: Douglas Baglin, Monkmeyer. 226–227: Grant Heilman. 228: Leonard Lee Rue III, Annan Photo Features. 229: (t) Des Bartlett, Bruce Coleman. 230: Karl Weidmann, National Audubon Society/Photo Researchers. 231: Esther Henderson, Rapho Guillumette/Photo Researchers. 232: Dick Robinson, Photo Researchers. 233: Josef Muench. 236: James Romeo, Photo Researchers. 237: (tl) Bruce Coleman; (tr) Ken Brate, National Audubon Society/Photo Researchers; (bl) Dan Sudia, Photo Researchers; (br) Ken Brate, National Audubon Society/Photo Researchers. 238: (tl) (tr) (bl) Dr. J. A. L. Cooke; (br) Dr. E. R. Degginger. 240: Keith Gunnar, Bruce Coleman. 241: (t) Hans Reinhard, Bruce Coleman; (c) Rapho Guillumette/Photo Researchers; (b) Douglas Baglin, Monkmeyer. 243: NASA.

ISBN 0-15-365734-0 PRINTED IN THE UNITED STATES OF AMERICA

Contents

	About This Book	1
1	Earth's Living Things—Animals	3
2	Earth's Living Things—Plants	31
3	Earth's Treasure—Soil	59
4	At Work on Earth	83
5	Earth in Space	129
6	Earth's Changing Forms	169
7	Fitness to Live	203
	Picture Reference: The Metric System	244
	Index of Key Concept Terms	246

About This Book

Will people ever live in colonies in space?

You know astronauts have lived and worked in space. In time there will be space stations. A space station will hold all that a colony of people needs. Its people will eat from the space station's store of food. They will drink from its store of water. They will breathe from its store of air. They will use electricity from its store of energy.

You are living in space. Your space station is planet Earth. You depend on your space station's stores.

Does Earth have plenty of these stores? What must we do to make Earth's stores last? To have plenty for all?

It is important to find out. We can begin by investigating. Scientists investigate. So will you, as you learn the ways of the scientists.

1/Earth's Living Things — Animals

It is under water. The parts like hairs wave slowly. It is called a sea anemone.

A small fish swims by. It touches the hairs. They sting. The fish cannot move. Is the sea anemone alive? If it is alive, is it a plant? Or is it an animal?

How do we know when something is alive? How do we know if it is a plant or an animal? Begin your probe on the next page.

1. Is It Alive?

Do you see anything that is alive here?

Do you see anything that is not alive?

You know that birds are alive. You know that trees are alive.

You know that rocks are not alive. But how do you know? How are birds and trees different from rocks?

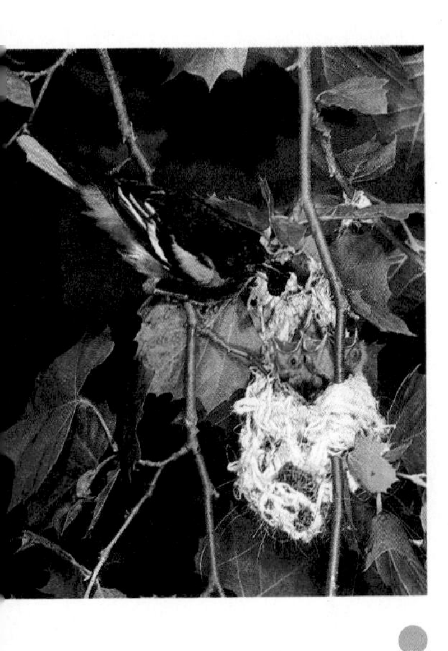

Birds grow. They lay eggs. Young birds hatch from the eggs. Birds make more birds, don't they? Birds reproduce. ●

Trees grow. They make seeds. Young trees grow from the seeds. Trees make more trees. Trees reproduce. ▲

Do rocks grow? No. Do rocks reproduce? No. That's how you know they are not alive.

●

Here's something else. Birds and trees need water to stay alive. They need food. They need air. Do rocks need these things?

▲

Rocks do not need water or food or air. Rocks are not alive. But living things need water and food and air to stay alive.

LOOK BACK

Look at these pictures. Which things are alive? Which things are not alive? Why do you say so?

ON YOUR OWN

Look around you. What living things do you see? Which things are not alive? Now, here is a tricky question. Do you see anything that came from a living thing?

2. The Right Place

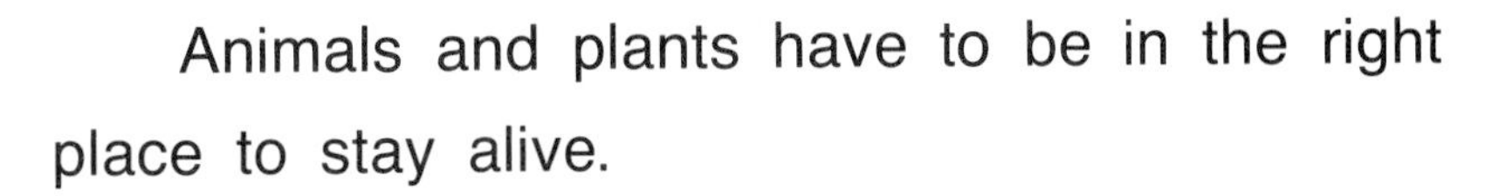

Animals and plants have to be in the right place to stay alive.

These plant seeds can grow. They can become radish plants like these.

The radish plants make more seeds. Radish plants make more radish plants. They reproduce.

But radish seeds don't turn into radish plants just anywhere. Animals and plants must have the right place to live.

What is the right place for a radish seed? Find out. Turn the page and INVESTIGATE.

LEARNING TO INVESTIGATE

The Right Place to Live

Needed: Six radish seeds, two sponges, two plates, water

Put one sponge on a plate. Pour a little water on the sponge to make it wet. ■

Put the other sponge on the other plate. Don't wet it. Keep it dry.

Put three radish seeds on the wet sponge. Put the other three seeds on the dry sponge. ●

Put the plates in a warm, shady spot. Add a little water to the wet sponge as it dries out. Keep it damp.

Look at your seeds each day. Look for signs of sprouting or growing. Here's what happened one time. ▲

Which seeds are in the right place to live? What do you think makes it the right place?

Where the Seeds Can Live

Radish seeds on the wet sponge start to grow. Seeds on the dry sponge do not grow.

To start to grow, a radish seed must have water. The right place for a radish seed to live is warm and damp. It must not be too hot or too cold. It must not be too wet or too dry.

A radish seed depends on what is around it, doesn't it? It depends on its surroundings, its environment. A radish seed must have a warm and damp environment. It must have the right environment to live.

This is true for all living things. What environment do these living things need?

Food for Living Things

Where does a radish seed get food? The seed has its own food supply. It starts to grow with that. When its own supply is used up, it makes food from the soil and from the air. It gets food from its environment.

A toad eats a moth. It gets food from the moth. ■

A snake eats a toad, and gets food. ●

A hawk eats a snake, and gets food. ▲

A living thing needs food. It must find the food in its environment, or it cannot live.

LOOK BACK

1. Which of the things in these pictures depend on their environment?
2. Which do not depend on their environment?
3. Which ones are living things?

USING WHAT YOU KNOW

Begin an Animal Scrapbook. Look in old newspapers and magazines. Cut out pictures of as many different kinds of animals as you can find.

ON YOUR OWN

The anemone on page 2 is not a plant. It is an animal. Can you find a picture of another animal that looks like a plant?

3. Sorting Living Things

Here are some living things. They all look different, don't they? But some are alike in being animals. Others are alike in being plants.

Can you sort these living things into animals and plants?

rose

Did you sort out ten animals and two plants? Now try sorting the animals. Sort them into groups called classes. Here are the classes.

fish class
reptile class
bird class
mammal class
amphibian class

Here is a hint. There will be two animals in each class. You can check out your classes on the next pages.

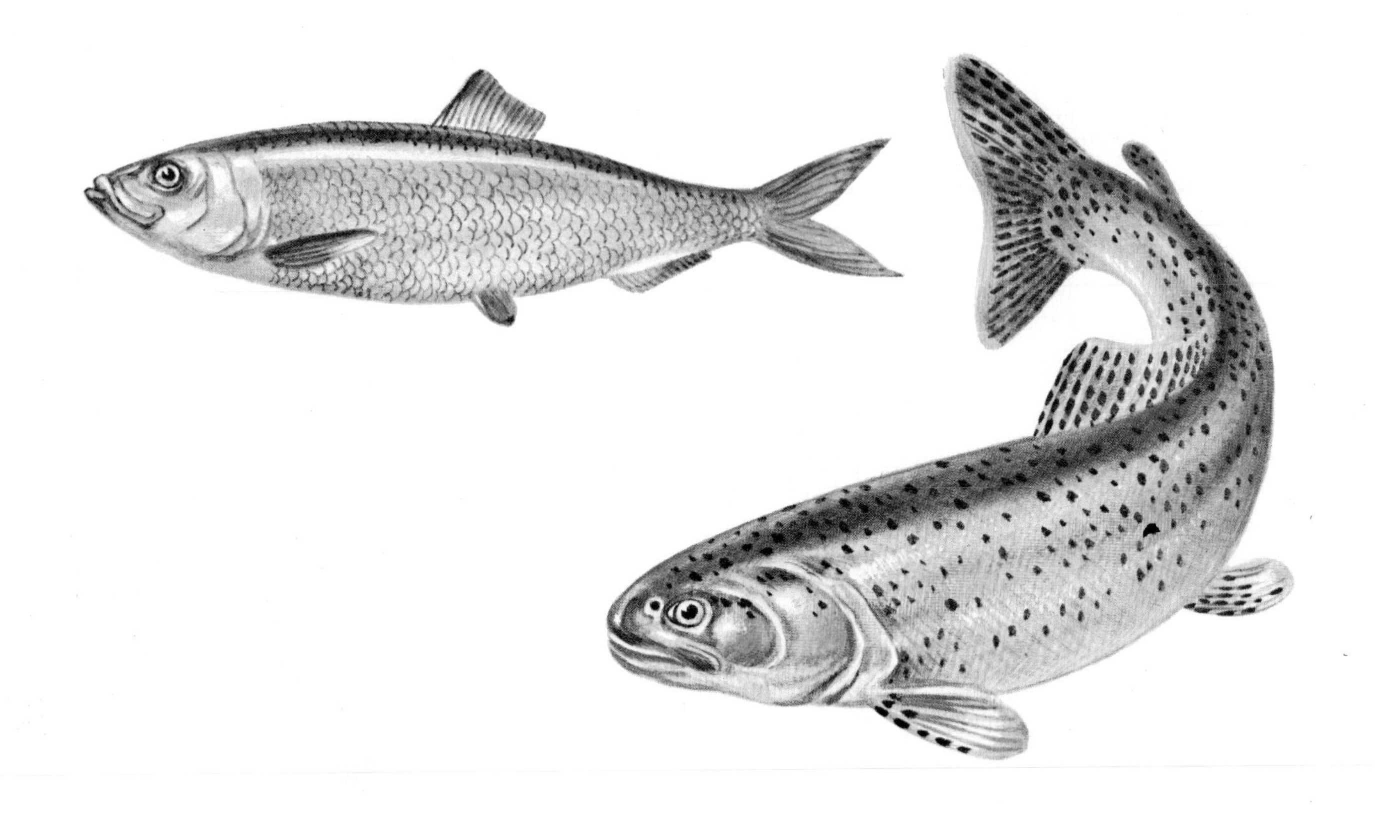

Fish—as a Class

Did you put the trout and the herring in the fish class?

Watch a goldfish under water. Its mouth opens and closes. It is breathing water.

The fish takes in some water through its mouth. Its gills take air from that water. Then it sends the water out, through slits just behind its head. The slits open and close too.

Can you find the slits on the trout? On the herring?

Amphibians—as a Class

The frog and the salamander are amphibians. Did you put them in the amphibian class?

An amphibian lives two lives, in a way. It lives the first part of its life in water. It may live the rest of its life on land.

A tadpole is a young amphibian. It takes air from the water. It swims like a fish. But as it grows it changes. It grows legs. It moves to the land. It breathes air. It becomes a frog.

The tadpole loses its tail as it grows older. The salamander keeps its tail!

Reptiles—as a Class

Did you put the snake and the lizard in the reptile class? That's where they go. So do turtles and alligators.

A reptile's body is covered with scales or with plates. You can see scales on the snake. The lizard has scales too. An alligator has plates.

Reptiles breathe air. Some spend most of their time in water. But they can't stay under water. They must come up for air.

Most reptiles reproduce by laying eggs. They lay their eggs on land. The eggshells are soft and tough, like leather.

Birds — as a Class

The goldfinch and the starling belong in the bird class.

There are many different kinds of birds. But they are all alike in some ways. They all breathe air. They all have two legs and two wings, and feathers. They all lay eggs with hard shells.

Any animal with feathers is sure to be a bird. But all birds cannot fly. The ostrich cannot fly. Its wings are too small. Can you think of another bird that cannot fly?

Mammals—as a Class

Where did you put the guinea pig and the mouse? They are mammals.

Most mammals do not lay eggs. Their young are born alive. Then the young are fed milk made in the mother's body.

All mammals breathe air. Nearly all mammals live on land. But whales are mammals that live in the sea. They must come up for air.

Nearly all mammals have hair or fur. A whale has a lot of bare skin. But most whales have a few hairs around their mouths or under their chins!

LOOK BACK

In which class does each of these belong? Why do you think so?

cat	canary	bear
garter snake	toad	dove
rabbit	sardine	horse

USING WHAT YOU KNOW

1. Have you saved animal pictures? If you have, you can begin your Animal Scrapbook. Make five sections for the five classes. Paste in pictures that belong in the five classes. Do you have some that don't seem to belong? Save them. You will learn about them later.

2. This animal is a bat. ■ It flies, but it is not a bird. It is a mammal. Does it have feathers? What do you think?

■

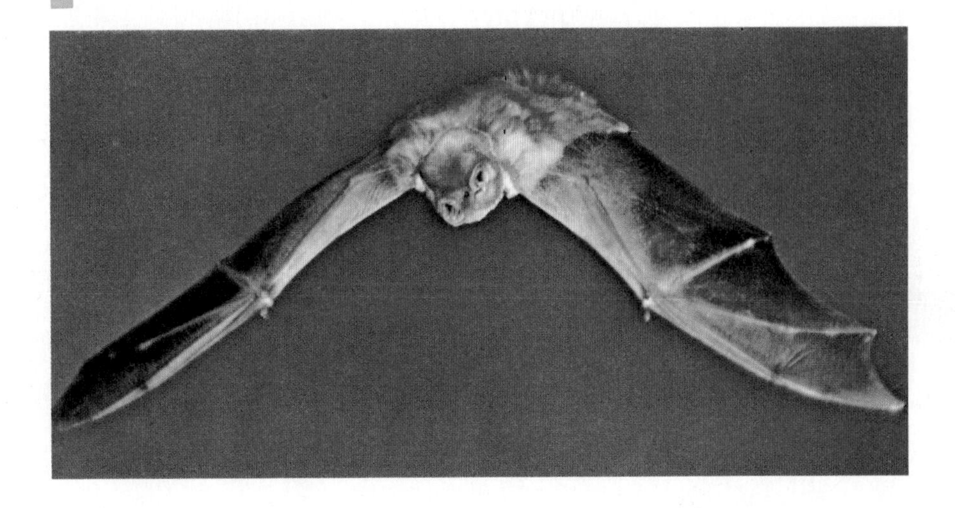

4. They Are Alike

You have studied five classes of animals. They do not look much alike, do they? Yet they are alike.

Here are five skeletons. There is a fish, an amphibian, a reptile, a bird, and a mammal. See if you can sort them out. ■

Now look at the part in red in each skeleton. It is a backbone. They all have backbones.

What is a backbone like? **INVESTIGATE**

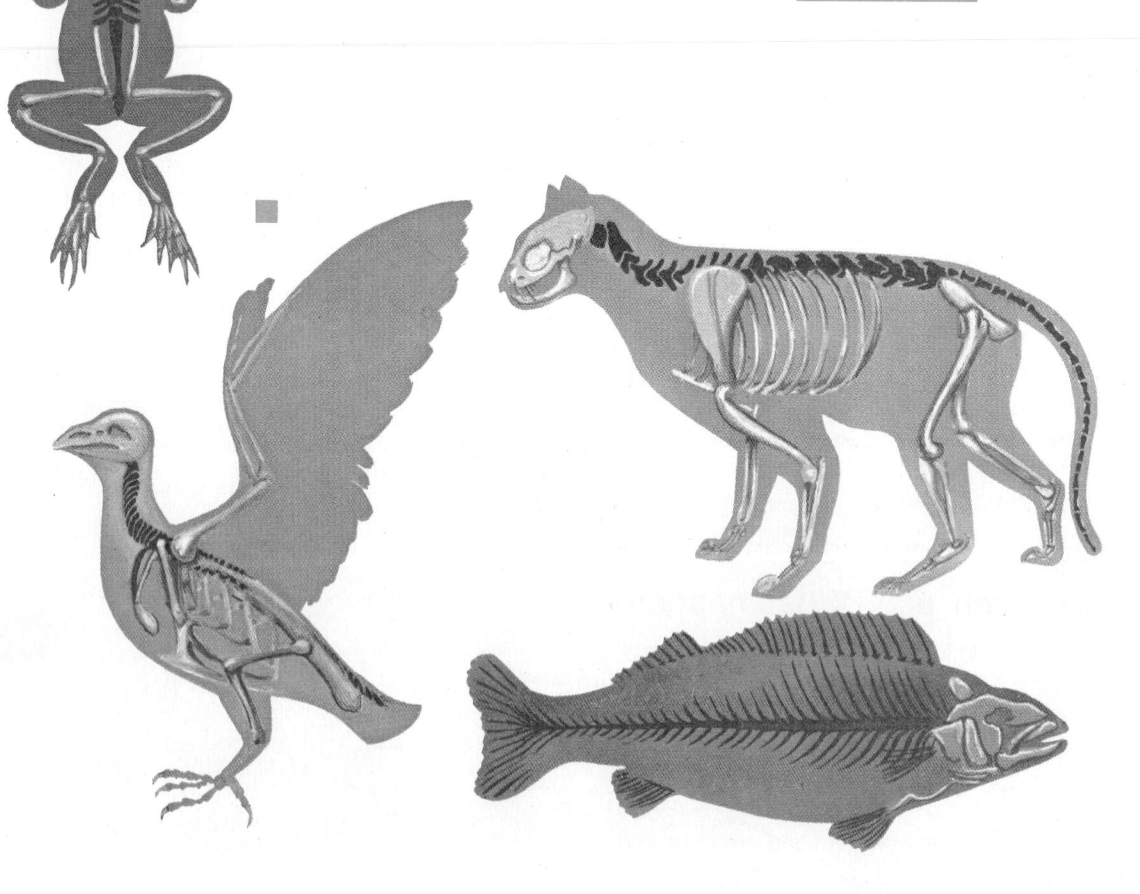

LEARNING TO INVESTIGATE

What Is a Backbone Like?

Needed: Four spools and a straw

Bend one end of the straw. ■

Slide the spools on the straw. Then press the lowest spool against the table. ●

Move the top spool over to one side a little. What happens? ▲

Do you notice that each spool tilts a little? But the little tilts add up. Because of this, the whole chain of spools can bend a lot.

A backbone is a chain of small bones. Each one can move a little. The whole backbone can move a lot.

Bend over. Can you feel the bones in your backbone? Now straighten up. What happens?

■

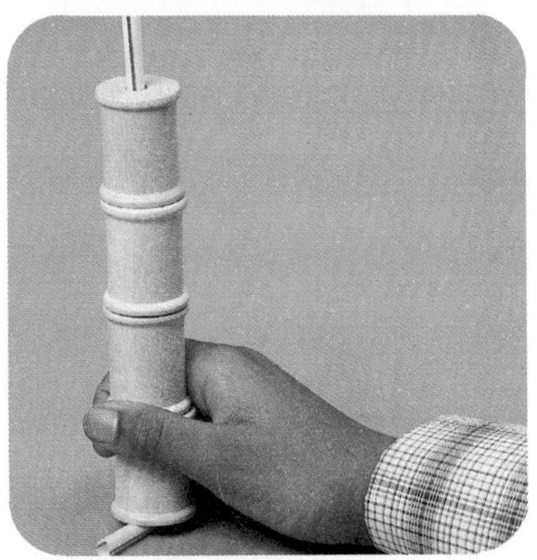

●

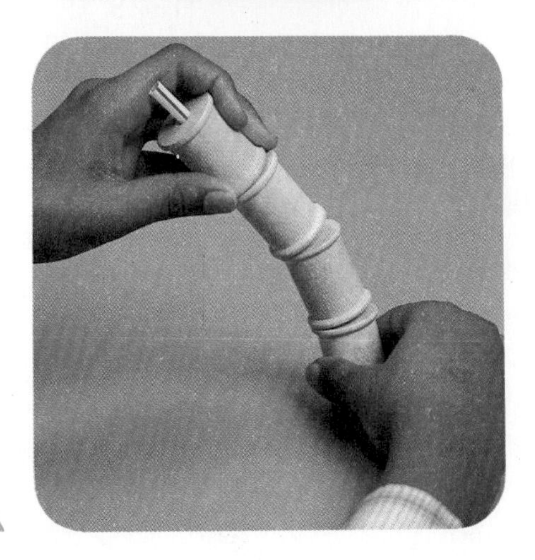

▲

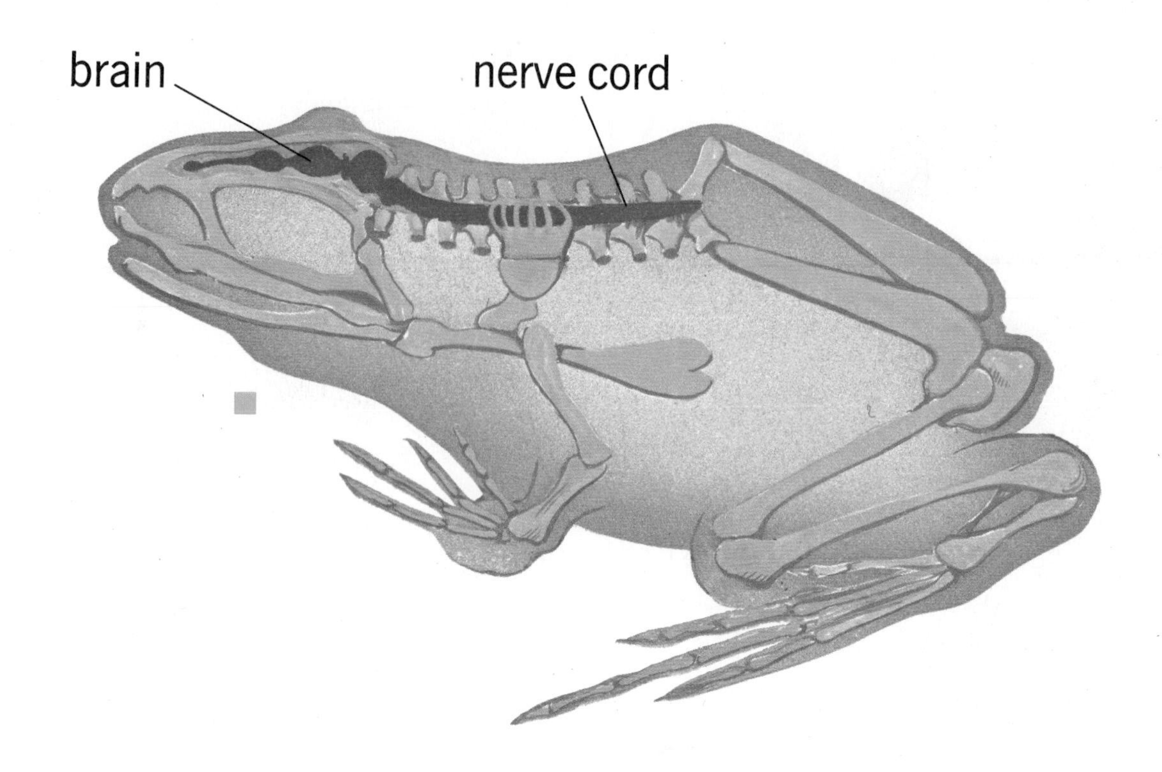

Animals With Backbones

Did you notice the holes in the bones of a backbone? The holes are for the nerve cord. The nerve cord is inside the backbone.

The nerve cord connects the brain with other parts of the body. Here are the nerve cord and the brain in a frog. ■

Animals with backbones are sometimes called vertebrates. There are many different kinds of vertebrates. How many can you name?

Are you wondering if there are animals *without* backbones? There are. We will look at them next.

Search on Your Own

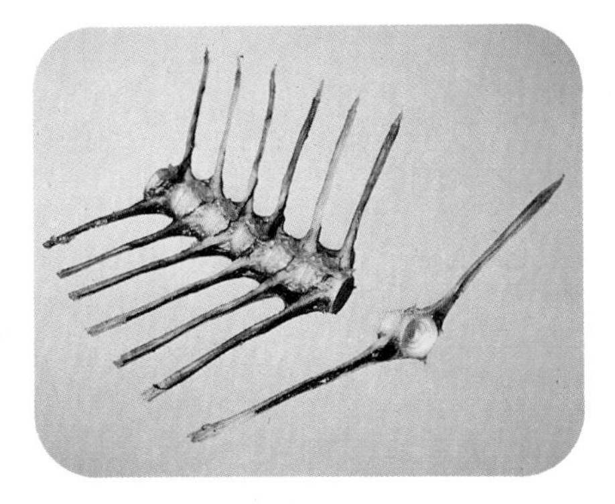

See if you can get a backbone. You may get one saved from a fish dinner. Place the bones of the backbone on a sheet of paper. Can you fit the small bones together? Can you make part of a backbone?

What happens when a fish bends its back? Can you show what happens?

LOOK BACK

Here is the skeleton of a snake. ● Is the snake a vertebrate? Why do you say so?

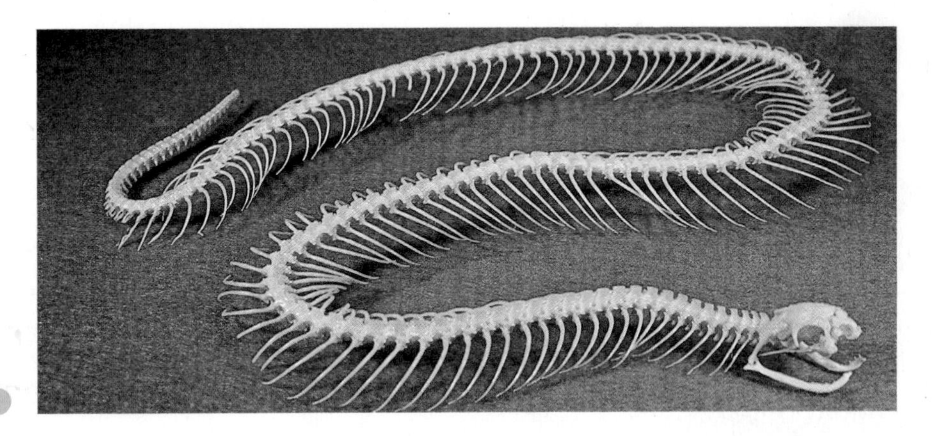

ON YOUR OWN

Some people can touch their toes without bending their knees. Could they do this if their backbones did not bend? What do you think?

5. Animals Without Backbones

You have put plants in one group. You have put animals in another group. You have put the animals in five classes.

Scientists call this classifying. You classify things when you put them in groups. Classifying is important in science. It is a way to sort things out.

You classified animals with backbones. But many kinds of animals have no backbones. Here is how some of them are classified.

Animals With Spiny Skins

These animals live in the sea. Most of them have rough skins with spines sticking out. Most of them reproduce by laying eggs.

sea urchin

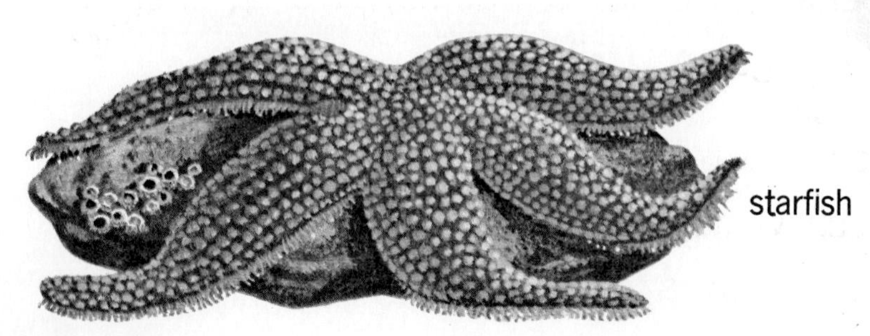

starfish

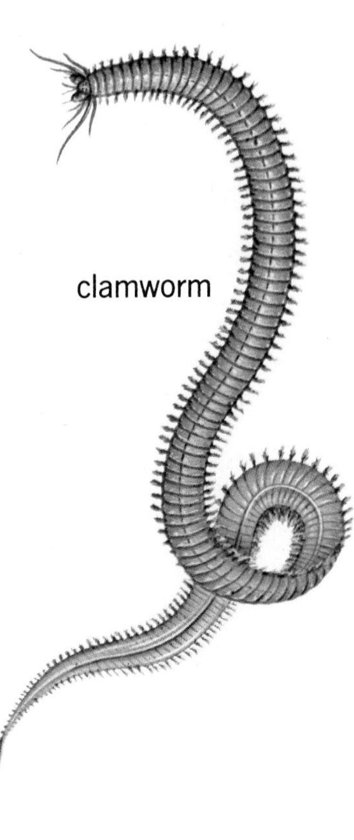

Ringed Worms

Some of these worms live on land. Some live in water. They lay eggs. Watch a worm move. The rings stretch out. Then they come together again.

You can keep earthworms in a box of moist garden soil. Feed them corn meal and bits of lettuce.

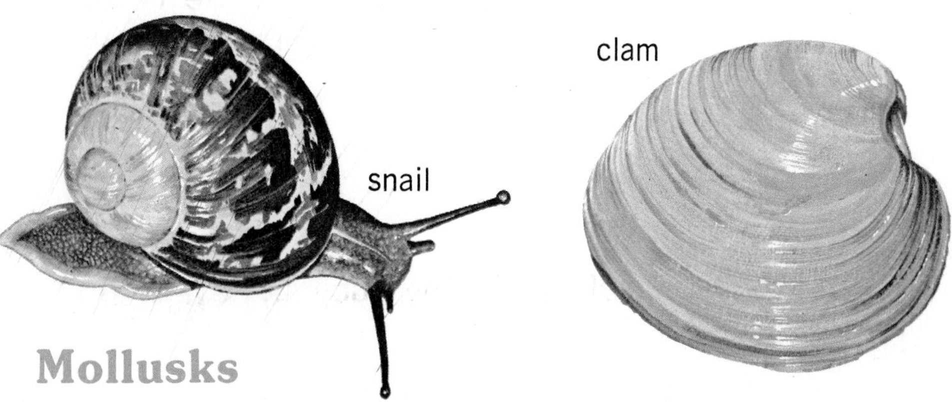

Mollusks

Mollusks have soft bodies. But most of them live in hard shells. They make the shells. Some make one-part shells, like snails. Some make two-part shells, like clams. Some have no shell at all, like slugs.

Most mollusks are sea animals. A few kinds live in fresh water or on land. You can raise pond snails in an aquarium.

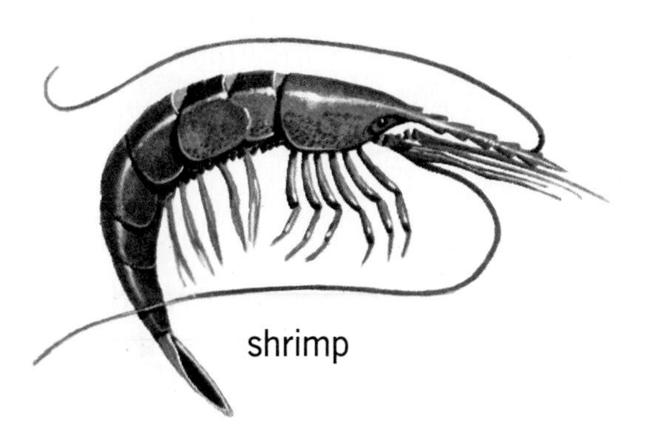

shrimp

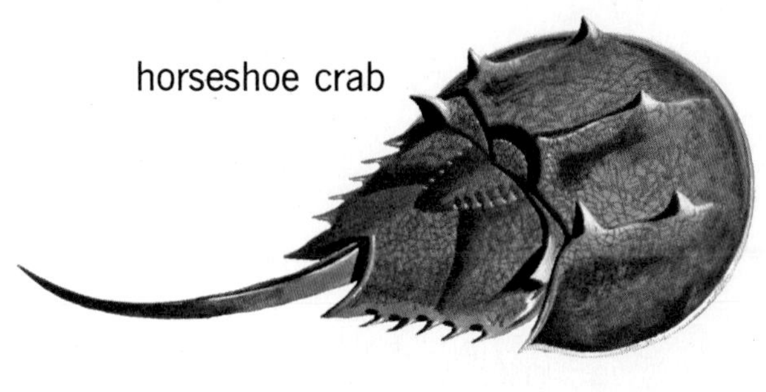

horseshoe crab

Animals With Jointed Legs

wood louse

There are many different kinds of animals in this group. But all of them have legs that bend at the joints. Their skeletons are outside their skin. They reproduce by laying eggs. Some live in the sea. Some live in fresh water. And some live on land.

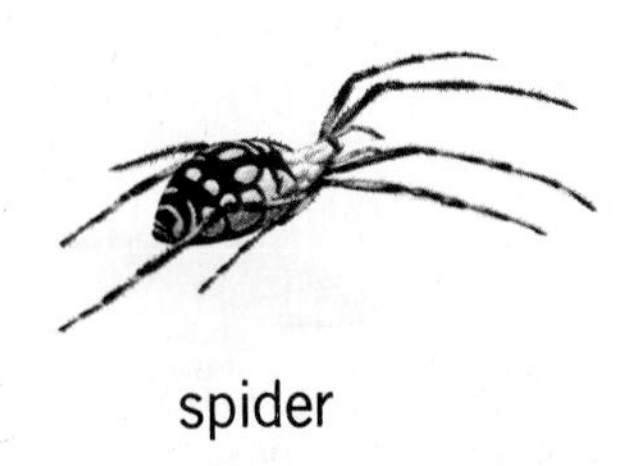

spider

Insects are the biggest class of animals with jointed legs. Some live on land, some live in fresh water. How can you tell an insect? An adult insect has six legs, two feelers, and a body in three parts.

swallowtail butterfly

housefly

Search on Your Own

What groups of animals live in your environment?

Look around you for vertebrates. Some are cared for by people. Some take care of themselves.

Look for animals that have no backbones. Look indoors as well as outdoors. Make a list.

LOOK BACK

How would you classify these animals? Why? Use pages 24 to 26.

1. The *oyster* lays eggs. It lives in the sea. It has a soft body inside a hard shell.
2. The *brittle star* lives in the sea. It has a rough, spiny skin.
3. The *grasshopper* has six jointed legs. Its body is in three parts.

Classifying is important in science because it sorts things out.

We classify things as alive or not alive. If a thing is alive, we know it depends on its environment. We know it can reproduce. It can make more living things like itself.

We classify living things as plants or animals. We classify animals. We put animals that have backbones, the vertebrates, in one group. We put animals without backbones in another group.

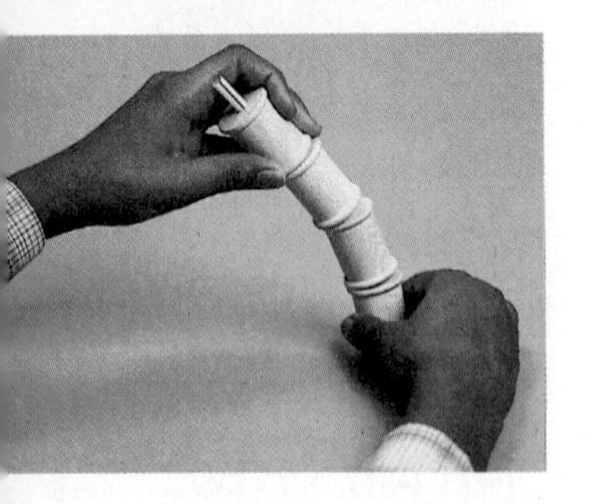

We classify vertebrates in five classes: fish, amphibian, reptile, bird, mammal. And we put animals without backbones into different groups.

Living things that are alike in some way can be put into a group.

1. Which of these needs air, water, and food?
2. Which ones grow?
3. Which can move around by themselves?
4. Which can reproduce?
5. How would you classify them?

2/ Earth's Living Things — Plants

The fly is looking for food. But it is about to become food.

Those two halves are coming together. In a moment the fly will be caught between them. It will not be able to escape. It will be used for food.

Is the fly being trapped by a hungry animal? Or by a hungry plant?

Animal or plant? What do you think?

1. The Plant Kingdom

We share the Earth with many living things. Some are animals. They belong to the animal kingdom. Some are plants, and belong to the plant kingdom. Here is a tiny part of the plant kingdom. ■

There are many different plants here, aren't there? Yet in one way most of them are alike. They are green in color.

Why are most plants green? There is a reason. See for yourself. **INVESTIGATE**

■

LEARNING TO INVESTIGATE

What Happens to a Green Leaf in the Dark?

Needed: Unused carbon paper, paper clips, an indoor plant

Fold carbon paper around two green leaves. Be sure it shuts out all light. Hold the paper on with paper clips. ■

■

Write the date on the pot. Put the plant in sunlight. Now two green leaves are in the dark. The rest are in the light.

After five days take the paper off one leaf. ●

●

What has happened to the leaf in the dark? Compare it with the leaves in the light.

After five more days take the paper off the other leaf. Compare it with the leaves that were in the light. ▲

▲

How do you explain what happens?

In the Dark

The leaves wrapped in paper are in the dark. They lose their bright green color. If they are kept in the dark, the leaves die. ■

■

They die from lack of food.

You see, a green leaf makes the food it needs. To make food the leaf must use its green stuff. The green stuff is chlorophyll.

But a leaf kept in the dark can't use its chlorophyll. Then the leaf cannot make food. It dies. If a green plant is kept in the dark, the whole plant dies.

It is chlorophyll that makes plants green. But that's not all. Chlorophyll helps plants make food.

LOOK BACK

Complete each sentence.

1. Plants and animals are grouped in two
   families   kingdoms

2. Green plants make their own
   water   food

3. A green leaf gets its color from
   chlorophyll   paper

4. Without chlorophyll a plant cannot
   make air   make food

5. A green leaf kept in the dark
   soon dies   becomes stronger

USING WHAT YOU KNOW

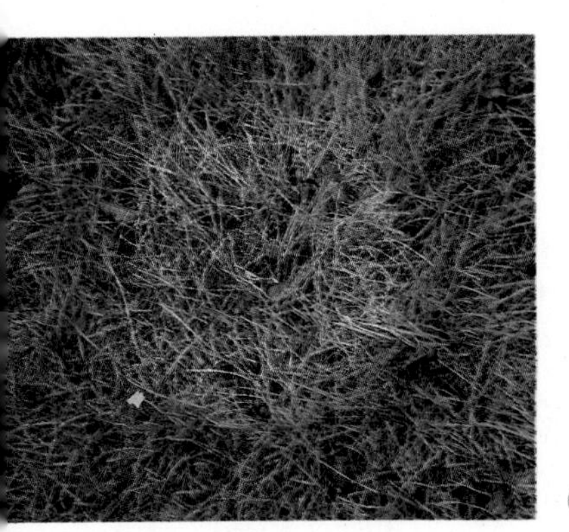

A pan was left on the grass one day. Some days later it was picked up. Here is how the grass under the pan looked. ●

What has happened? How did it happen?

ON YOUR OWN

Are all green leaves the same shade of green? What other colors can you find in leaves?

2. Living Without Chlorophyll

Do you see green in these mushrooms?

These mushrooms have no green. Mushrooms have no chlorophyll in them.

There are other plants without chlorophyll. But doesn't a plant need chlorophyll to make food? How can a plant without chlorophyll get food? How can it live and grow?

You can find out. Raise some plants of your own. Raise some mold plants. Mold plants have no chlorophyll. **INVESTIGATE**

LEARNING TO INVESTIGATE

Where Do Mold Plants Grow?

Needed: A piece of fresh bread, a piece of very dry toast, two plastic bags, string

Leave the pieces of bread and toast uncovered all night.

Next day put the piece of bread in one bag. Put the piece of toast in the other bag.

Put five or six drops of water on the piece of bread. Do not put any water on the toast.

Tie the bags tightly. ■

Now put the two bags in a warm, dark cupboard. Look at them every day. But don't open them. Look for mold. Does it grow on the bread? ● On the toast? ▲

How do you explain what happens?

When you have finished, don't open the bags. Throw them out.

Mold Plants and Food

Mold plants grow on the bread. They do not grow on the toast. Why? Because mold plants need water. The bread has water. The toast is dry. It has no water.

Mold plants need food. Here is how they get it. Look at the mold plants through a magnifying glass. You will see many tiny threads. Some grow upward and have little balls on top. ■

But you will notice that some of the tiny threads go right into the bread. They take food from the bread. The mold plants growing on the bread get their food from the bread.

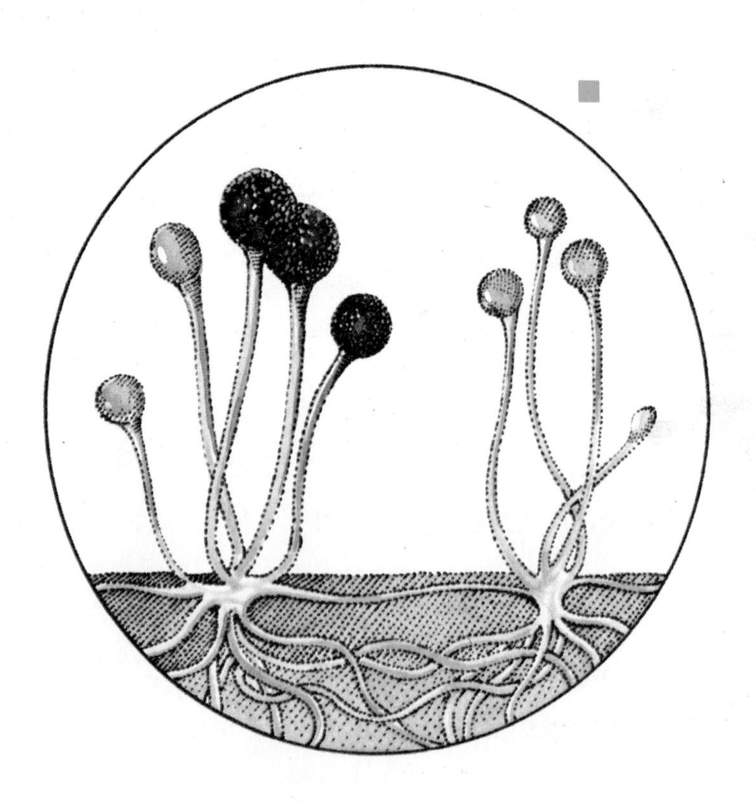

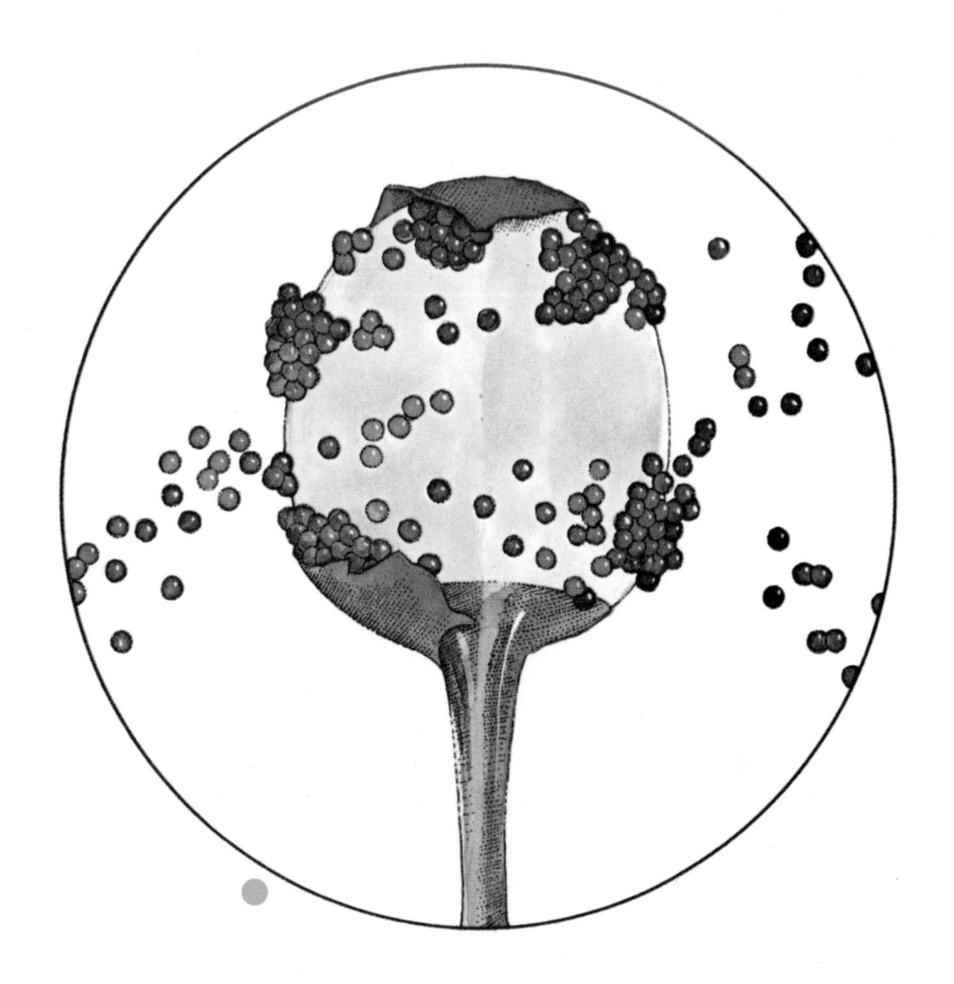

That little ball on top of a thread is about the size of a pinhead. The ball is a spore case. Inside the spore case are thousands of spores. When the spore case is ripe, it pops open. Out come the spores.

The spores are carried along in the air. Some may land on bread. Some may land on fruit, or other food. Many spores stay in the air.

Some of the spores land where they can live. They grow into more mold plants. Mold plants reproduce from spores.

How Mushrooms Reproduce

The threads of a mushroom plant are underground. Small buttons grow on the threads. ■

A button grows upward. ● It gets bigger. ▲ The cap opens like an umbrella. ◆

The cap is filled with thousands of spores. When the plant is ripe, the spores fall out. ★

Some spores fall where they can live. They become new mushroom plants.

Living Without Chlorophyll

Mushrooms have no chlorophyll. Molds have no chlorophyll. Many other plants have no chlorophyll. They all belong to a group called fungi. Fungi cannot make food. Fungi get food some other way.

Molds are fungi. Molds that grow on bread get food from the bread. Molds that grow on fruit get food from the fruit. Mushrooms are fungi. Mushrooms that grow in soil get food from the soil. These fungi are getting their food from a living tree.

Fungi are plants without chlorophyll.

LOOK BACK

1. Fungi are
   animals   plants

2. Fungi have no
   spores   chlorophyll

3. Fungi cannot make
   food   spores

4. Mold plants can get food from
   sunlight   bread

5. Mold plants reproduce by
   spores   eggs

USING WHAT YOU KNOW

In the investigation on page 37, you grew mold plants. But first the bread was left uncovered for a while. If this is not done, mold may not grow.

Why must the bread be left uncovered for a while?

3. With Seeds and Without Seeds

Let's begin with an apple tree in spring. The tree is covered with flowers. ■ Bees come to the flowers. ●

■

●

Soon the petals of the flowers fall off. Small green balls grow where the flowers were. The balls are little green apples. ▲

The apples grow. Their color changes. Before the end of summer they are ripe. ◆

And inside each apple are seeds. ★

How do seeds begin? Find out. Look in a flower. **INVESTIGATE**

▲

◆

★

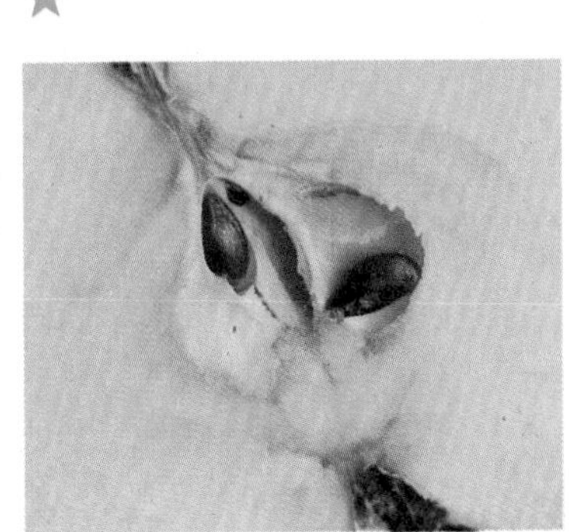

LEARNING TO INVESTIGATE

What Is Inside a Flower?

Needed: A lily or a tulip, and a magnifying glass

Pull off some petals. Then you can look at a stamen. Use the magnifying glass. ■

■

Do you see a kind of dust on the stamen? It is pollen. Touch the stamen. You will find some pollen on your finger.

Use the magnifying glass to look at the pistil. ●

●

Touch the top of the pistil. Does it feel sticky? Suppose pollen lands on the sticky part. Then the pollen sticks to the pistil.

At the bottom of the pistil there is a thick part. Split it open with your fingernail. You will see rows of things like tiny beads. ▲

▲

Take another big flower apart. Do you find the same parts?

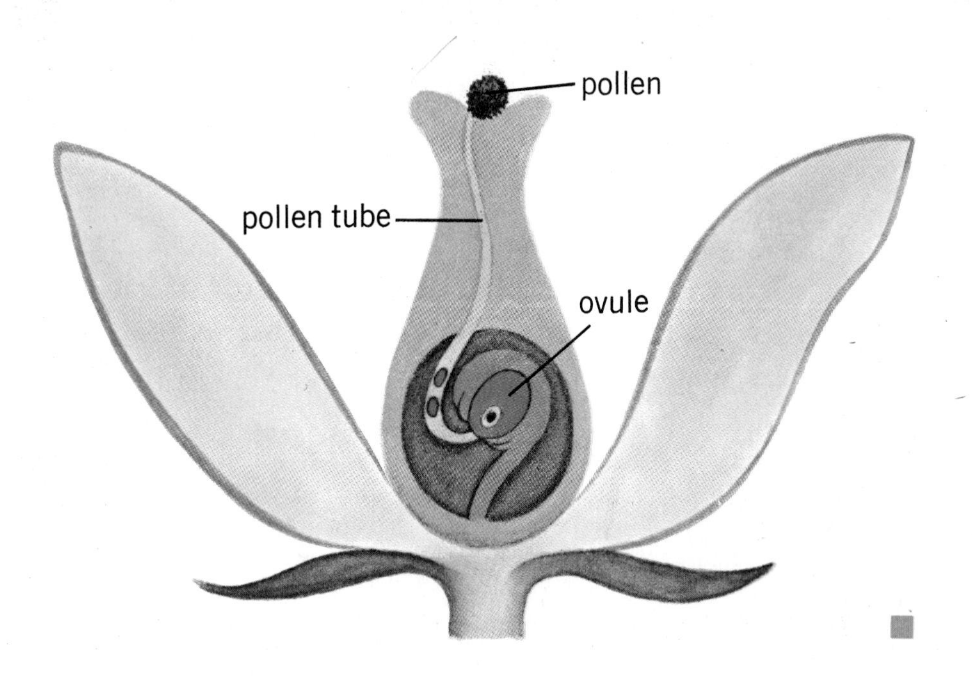

How Seeds Are Made

A bee flies from flower to flower. It is getting food. But the hairs on its body pick up pollen from a flower. Some of that pollen sticks to the pistil of the next flower. That flower is pollinated.

When a flower is pollinated, here's what happens. A tiny bit of pollen sticks to the pistil of the flower. ■

A tube grows from the bit of pollen. The tube goes down into the pistil. It goes into an ovule, one of the tiny round things like beads. The ovule grows into a seed.

The pistil gets bigger and bigger. It becomes a fruit. Inside the fruit are the plant's seeds.

■

Seeds Without Flowers

A flowering plant has fruit. Inside the fruit are seeds. But there are plants that have no flowers. Yet they have seeds!

Think of a tree with cones, such as a pine tree. It never has flowers. ■

But it has two kinds of cones. It has pollen cones. They have pollen. And it has seed cones. They have ovules. ●

Wind carries pollen from pollen cones to seed cones. When pollen reaches the ovules, they grow into seeds. When the seeds are ripe, the seed cones open. The seeds fall out. ▲

◆

Without Seeds

Do you ever see plants like these? They are ferns. ◆

★

Ferns have roots and stems and leaves. They have chlorophyll and make their food. But ferns do not have flowers. Or seeds. Or fruits.

Look at the dots on these fern leaves. ★

The dots are spore cases. A spore case opens when its spores are ripe. The spores fall out. Some land where they can grow. They make new fern plants.

Search on Your Own

What flower plants live near you? What trees with cones can you find? Can you find any ferns?

Can you find any plants without chlorophyll?

Draw pictures of plants you find. Or take photographs. Pick out one plant and watch it grow and change. Make a record once a week of the changes you see.

LOOK BACK

1. A fruit has
seeds flowers

2. New fern plants grow from
seeds spores

3. Trees that have cones have no
seeds flowers

4. To make seeds, a flower must be
in the wind pollinated

5. Pollen sticks to the tip of a
pistil seed

USING WHAT YOU KNOW

Make a big drawing of a flower. Show the parts of the flower. Color the petals, stamens, pollen, and pistil. Label the parts. And show where the ovules are.

The pictures of flowers on pages 44 and 45 will help you.

ON YOUR OWN

You may enjoy growing some plants. Why not find out? It is easy to begin.

Fill a flowerpot with soil from a garden. Water the soil. Make it damp, but not muddy. Then fit a clean jar over the soil.

You now have a little greenhouse. Stand it in a warm place with plenty of light.

In a few days, you will see little plants coming up even though you did not plant any seeds.

How did they get started? Try to explain what happens in your greenhouse.

4. With Tubes and Without Tubes

Trees are the biggest and oldest living things on Earth.

One of the biggest trees is this sequoia in California. ■ It is 30 stories high and nearly 4,000 years old.

Leaves grow on top of this giant. They get water from the soil far below. How does the water get up to the leaves? It travels through tubes in the tree trunk.

■

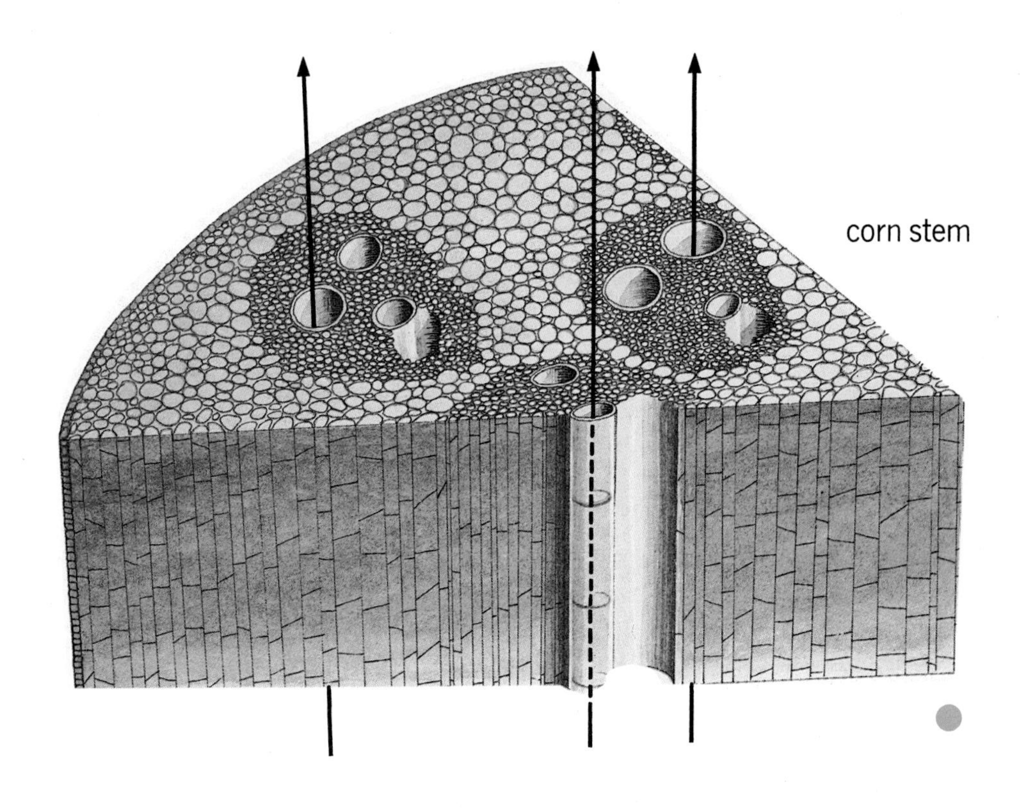

Plants With Tubes

Water travels to the top of that big old sequoia through tubes. The apple tree has tubes. Trees that have seeds have tubes.

Grass has tubes. Garden flowers have tubes. Plants that have seeds have tubes.

Ferns do not have seeds. Ferns grow from spores, you remember. But ferns have tubes.

Look for hollow tubes in grass stems. Look for them in a stalk of celery. Look in other plant stems. Most green plants have tubes. But there are plants *without* tubes.

Plants Without Tubes

Have you ever seen moss? It grows in the woods and in damp, shady places.

Moss plants have chlorophyll. They make food. But they have no flowers or seeds. They never grow tall. They have no tubes. They stay close to where the water is.

There are other plants without tubes. This green patch on a pond is made of tiny algae.

Algae are green plants without tubes. There are many kinds. Seaweeds are large algae.

Seaweeds do not need tubes to carry water. Seaweeds live in water.

Classifying Plants

Scientists classify plants. They sort plants into groups. Plants that are alike in some important way go into the same group.

Scientists used to put all the plants with seeds in one group. They put plants without seeds in another group. They put ferns in the group without seeds. Can you tell why? ▲

But scientists now classify plants in a new way. They put plants with tubes in one group, and plants without tubes in another group. So ferns are now in the same group as plants with seeds. They all have tubes in their stems. So do most of Earth's green plants.

▲

Search on Your Own

How does water get up to the top of a tree? Here is a clue.

Put a little water in a glass. Take a strip of paper towel. If you fold it as shown in the photo, it will stand up by itself. Put one end in the water. Let the strip stand in the water for a few minutes.

Watch what happens.

How do you think it happens?

LOOK BACK

1. Water moves to the top of a tree in
   spores   tubes
2. Most kinds of green plants have
   tubes   no tubes
3. One kind of plant without tubes is a
   fern   moss
4. One kind of plant with tubes is
   algae   grass
5. Seaweeds do not need tubes because they
   do not use water   live in water

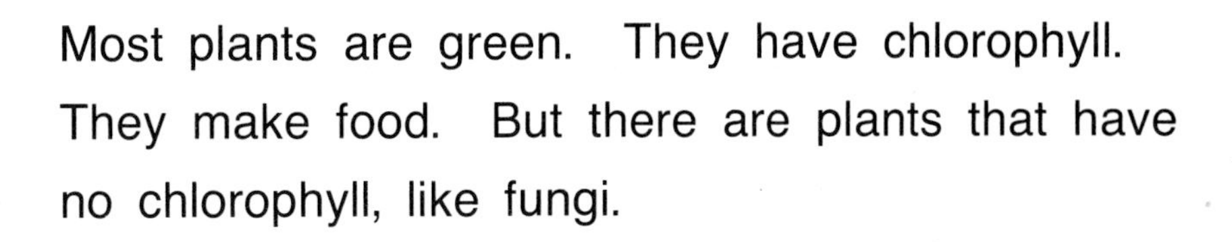

Most plants are green. They have chlorophyll. They make food. But there are plants that have no chlorophyll, like fungi.

Most kinds of green plants grow from seeds. And most plants with seeds have flowers. But some have cones.

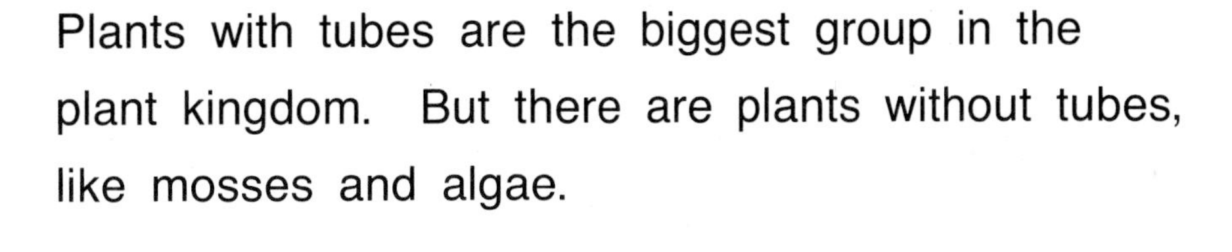

Plants with tubes are the biggest group in the plant kingdom. But there are plants without tubes, like mosses and algae.

Flowering plants, plants with cones, ferns, mosses, algae, fungi—how different they are! Yet they are also alike. They are living things. They all grow and reproduce. And they all depend on Earth's materials.

Plants have ways of making more of their own kind. They depend on their environment.

mold

algae

pansy

pine

moss

fern

Answer these questions about the pictures.

1. Which is a plant with cones?
2. Which is a plant with tubes?
3. Which plants have chlorophyll?
4. Which plant has flowers?
5. Which cannot make food?
6. Which green plant grows from spores?

Which picture fits each sentence?

7. These fungi cannot make food.
8. These plants can live in water.
9. Plants that have flowers have seeds.
10. This plant has seeds and no flowers.
11. This plant cannot grow tall.

3/Earth's Treasure — Soil

Both hands hold soil. But one soil is rich. Plants can grow in it.

The other soil is poor. It is worn out. Plants cannot live in it.

How does this happen? What makes one soil rich? What makes another soil poor? Does it matter?

It matters. See for yourself. Begin on the next page.

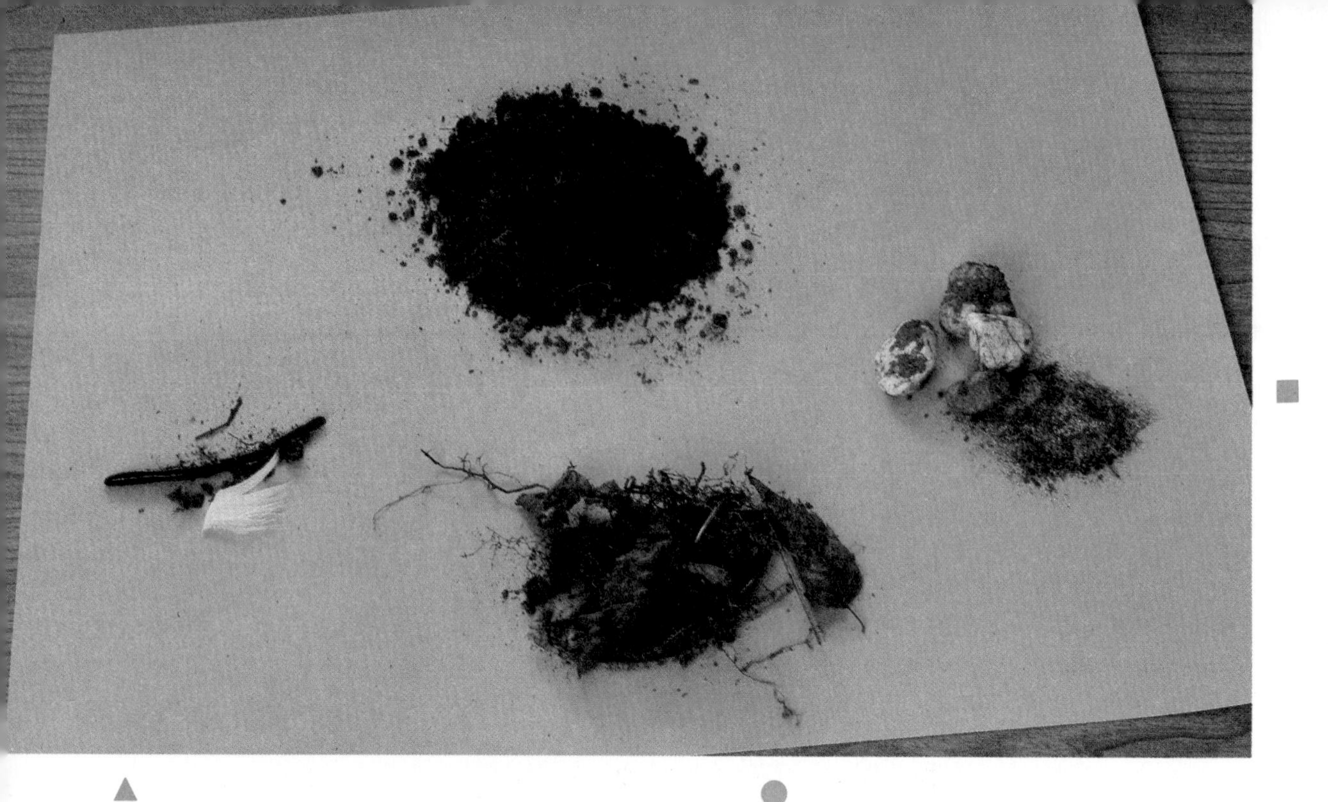

■ ▲ ●

1. What Is Soil?

What is the stuff we call soil?

Dig up a cupful of garden soil. Spread half your soil on a paper. Observe bits of it through a magnifying glass.

Look for pebbles. Look for tiny stones. Look for bits of sand and clay. These materials are from rock. ■

Look for bits of wood and bark. Look for roots, stems, seeds. These are from plants. ●

Now look for materials from animals. Bones. Snail shells. Feathers. Ants. Earthworms. Look for other small animals, living or dead. ▲

You may not find all of these in your soil. You may find other things. But good garden soil is made of two main kinds of materials:

—materials from rock

—materials from living things.

As time passes, materials from living things break down. They fall apart. They decay. As they decay, they make humus. Humus is made from parts of decayed plants and animals. ♦

Soil has humus in it. Soil has materials from rock in it. What else is in it? **INVESTIGATE**

♦

LEARNING TO INVESTIGATE

Is There Water in Your Soil?

Needed: Half cupful of garden soil, glass cooking pot with lid, electric hot plate, teacher in charge

■

Put the soil into the pot. Put the pot on the hot plate. ■

Cover the pot with the lid. Ask your teacher to turn the heat to *medium.*

●

As the soil is heated, observe the sides and the lid, carefully. Do you see anything collecting there? What do you think it may be? ●

Ask your teacher to turn off the hot plate. Let the pot cool.

▲

When the pot is cool, examine the inside of the lid. What do you find there? What does it look like? What does it feel like? ▲

Where do you think it comes from? How do you explain it?

LEARNING TO INVESTIGATE

Are There Other Things in Your Soil?

Needed: Two clean glass jars, rubber band, paper towel, clean glass pie pan, half cupful of garden soil, water

■

First make a filter. Push the paper towel into the jar to make a kind of bag—a filter. Hold it with the rubber band. ■

●

Mix the soil and some water in the other jar. Pour the mixture into the filter. What goes through the filter? ●

Pour the liquid that went through the filter into the pie pan. Set the pan aside for a few days. Let the water evaporate.

When the pan is dry, feel it. What you find there came from your soil. What do you think it is? ▲

▲

Most soil has water in it. When you heat the soil in a pot, the water comes out. Drops of water from the soil collect on the lid and sides of the pot.

Soil has other things in it. You put filtered water in a pan. You let the water evaporate. But something is left in the pan. You can see it and feel it. It is a thin layer of minerals. Plants need minerals. They can get them from soil.

Most soil has air in it. The air is in the spaces between bits of soil. When it rains, water goes down into the soil through these spaces. ■

LOOK BACK

1. Sand and clay are from
   plants — rock

2. Living things that decay
   break down — build up

3. Humus comes from
   rock — living things

4. Most soil has
   water in it — no water in it

5. Plants need
   filters — minerals

PLANNING AHEAD

You may soon want to observe some radish plants. Now is a good time to start them growing.

Fill three small flowerpots with damp soil. Put six radish seeds in each pot. Follow the directions on the package of seeds. ●

Keep the soil damp but not muddy. When the plants push up, give them plenty of light.

●

2. Soil as a Sponge

Lay a sponge in water. Then pick it up and squeeze it. ■

A sponge can hold water. So can most soils. Most soils hold onto water like a sponge. But there are different kinds of soils. Some soil is mainly sand. Some soil is mainly humus. Humus is decayed material, you remember.

Do some soils hold more water than others? That could be important for plants. What do you think? INVESTIGATE

■

LEARNING TO INVESTIGATE

Do Soils Differ in Holding Water?

Needed: Three coffee cans, three clear jars, hammer and large nail, water, measuring cup, one cupful each of sand, garden soil, humus soil

■

Use the hammer and nail to make six holes in the bottom of each can. Make the holes halfway between middle and edge. ■

Put the cupful of sand in the first can. Put the cupful of garden soil in the next can. Put the cupful of humus soil in the last can. Label the cans.

●

Put a jar under each can. Then pour exactly one cup of water into each can. ●

Which can lets the most water run through? ▲

Which material holds back the most water?

▲

In the Woods

Humus soil is a good sponge. It soaks up water. These trees are growing in humus soil.

Trees grow well in this soil. So do other plants. They get plenty of water from the soil. Rabbits, mice, and squirrels eat the plants. So do some birds.

Hunting animals live here too. Foxes hunt here. So do owls and other birds that eat meat.

Do you see the dead trees and dead leaves on the ground? Animals also fall to the ground when they die. These plants and animals decay as time passes. They make humus soil.

On the Desert

Sandy soil is a poor sponge. It cannot hold much water. This desert in California has sandy soil. ▲

Rain may fall here only once in two years! And there is no spongy humus to soak up the water and hold it.

What plants live here? Plants that do not need much water. There are fewer living things here than in the woods. There are fewer things to decay and make humus soil.

▲

LOOK BACK

Use *sandy soil* or *humus soil* to answer each question.

1. Which soil holds more water?

2. Which soil is better for a plant from the woods?

3. Which soil has more materials from living things?

4. Which soil is better for a desert plant?

ON YOUR OWN

Make some soil! Use materials like these:

sand	dead flowers	old snail shells
clay	old bark	dead insects
tiny pebbles	dead leaves	old grass

Crush and mix the materials you get. Add water to make your soil damp. Will seeds sprout in your soil? Will plants grow in it?

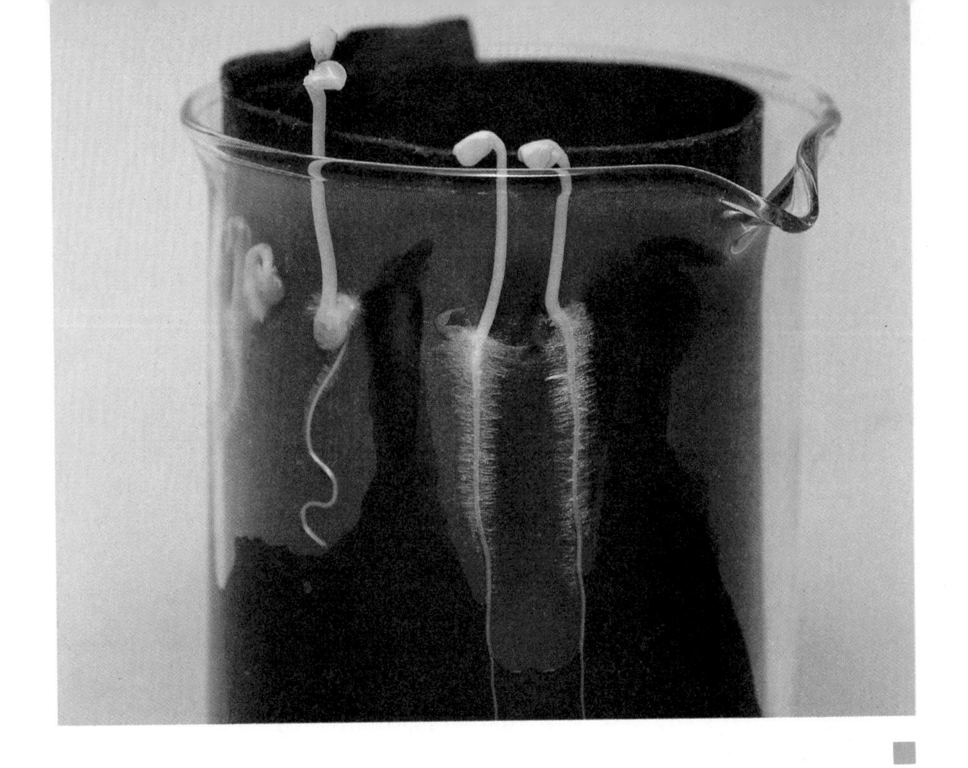

3. The Needs of Plants

Water soaks into soil. Soil has minerals in it, remember. Some of the minerals get into the water.

Plants need those minerals. How do plants get them? Take a magnifying glass. Look at the root of a young radish plant. Do you see tiny hairs? ■

Those hairs are called root hairs. Root hairs take in water. They take in minerals in the water. A plant gets water and minerals through its root hairs.

Then what happens to the water and minerals? You can see for yourself. **INVESTIGATE**

LEARNING TO INVESTIGATE

What Happens to Water and Minerals in a Plant?

Needed: Red or blue food coloring, a glass of water, a pale stalk of celery with leaves

Add the food color to the water. Make a bright color.

Look closely at the celery stalk and leaves. What color are they? Then cut off the bottom of the stalk. Stand the stalk in the colored water. ■

Observe the stalk about every hour for the rest of the day. Look for changes in the color of the stalk. Look for changes in the leaves too. One stalk looked like this after one hour. ●

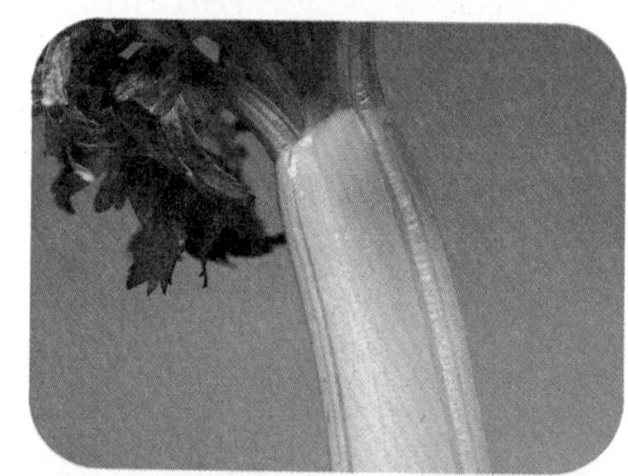

Its leaves looked like this after two hours. ▲

What changes do you observe? How do you explain them?

The colored water rises in the celery stalk. It goes up the stalk and into the leaves. Water with minerals in it rises the same way in a plant.

What else do plants need? Here are two healthy plants. They are growing well in sunlight. They have everything they need. ■

What will happen if one is put in a dark place? It will still have good soil, and plenty of water and air. But it will get no light. What differences will this make?

■

What Else Do Plants Need?

After a few days the two plants look like this. ■

The plant that had sunlight is growing well. But the one that stayed in the dark is turning white. It is losing its green chlorophyll. And it is starving. It cannot make its food.

Put the starving plant back in sunlight. It becomes green again! Its chlorophyll comes back. It starts making its food again.

Green plants need good soil, water, air, and minerals. But they need light too. Green plants use light to make their food.

Search on Your Own

Use three pots of young radish plants.

Can these plants get too much water? Plan an investigation.

You might keep the soil damp, but not muddy, in one pot.

Give the second pot more water every day.

Give the third pot much more water every day.

Keep everything else the same for all pots.

LOOK BACK

1. What happens to minerals in soil when it rains?
2. What are root hairs?
3. How do minerals get from soil into a plant?
4. What happens to a green plant kept in the dark?
5. What does a green plant need to grow?

4. Good Soil and Poor Soil

Fill one pot with clean, white sand. Fill another with garden soil. Plant four zinnia seeds in each pot. Put the pots in a warm, sunny spot. Keep the sand and the soil damp. In a few weeks the plants look like this. ■

Which plants look more healthy?

All the plants get plenty of light, air, and water. But the plants in one pot are not getting enough minerals. They are in poor soil.

■

Making Poor Soil Better

Poor soil does not have enough of the minerals that plants need.

But poor soil can be made better. Plant and animal materials can add minerals to the soil. These materials decay. They can change poor soil to good soil.

You can buy fertilizers that put minerals into the soil. This cotton crop is growing well. ● As it grows, it takes minerals from the soil. Good farmers put the same kind of minerals back into the soil. They know what fertilizers to use.

Using Our Soil Wisely

Soil is one of our greatest treasures. It must be used wisely. It must be conserved.

Earth has great deserts. Some of this dry desert soil is rich in minerals. It could be used for farming. We must get water to this dry soil.

Earth has places where water is washing away good soil. We can do things to save that soil. We can conserve it. ■

Good soil may be covered by buildings. It may be hidden under roads and parking lots. Look around you. Are we using our soil wisely? What do you think?

LOOK BACK

1. When is soil good?
2. When is soil poor?
3. How do you make poor soil better?
4. How do you conserve soil?
5. How do you use soil wisely?

ON YOUR OWN

Find a place where fertilizers are sold. It may be the plant department in a supermarket. It may be a plant or flower shop.

What are different fertilizers used for? What are they made from? Read the labels and find out.

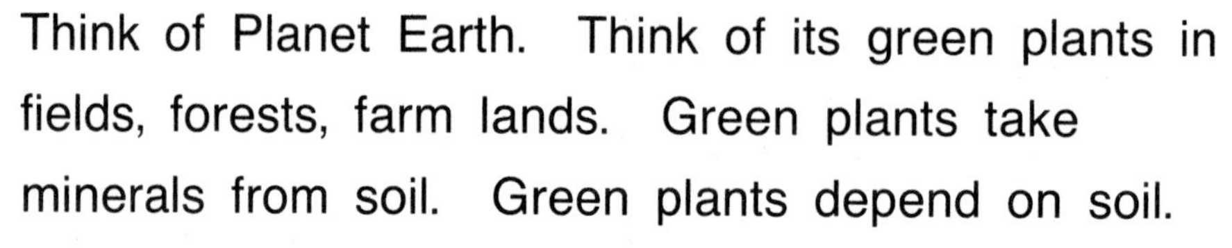

Think of Planet Earth. Think of its green plants in fields, forests, farm lands. Green plants take minerals from soil. Green plants depend on soil.

Think of Earth's many animals. They too need minerals. They get minerals from their food. They feed on green plants. They feed on animals that feed on green plants. Animals too depend on soil.

Think of Earth's people. We need minerals. We get minerals from food. Our food comes from green plants. It comes from animals that feed on green plants. We too depend on Earth's soil.

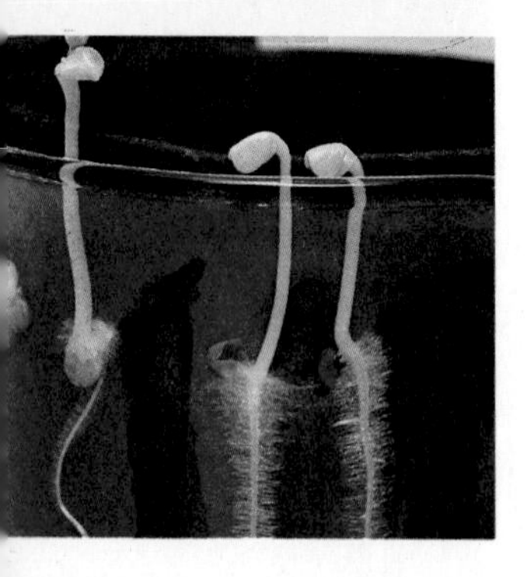

If soil is not conserved, what will happen?
What will happen to land plants?
What will happen to land animals?
What will happen to people?

All Earth's land plants and land animals depend on soil.

How do these foods depend on soil?

How do these things depend on soil?

4/At Work On Earth

He's pulling hard, isn't he?

It takes a lot of force to lift those weights. A force is a push or a pull. You use a force when you pull a drawer open. You use another force when you push the drawer shut.

Do you think he is working hard, trying to lift the weights? Well, a scientist would say that's not work at all!

Let's see why.

1. Doing Work

It rains hard. Leaves fall from the trees. Then the rain stops and people come out again. A girl sweeps up leaves.

She pushes the leaves off the sidewalk. She is using a force. A force is a push or a pull, remember. She is using her force to move leaves.

Is she doing work, do you think?

Is the girl doing work? You say yes right away, don't you? But a scientist would stop and think. Scientists have a special idea about work. Scientists say work is done when a force makes something move.

Is a force making something move? Yes, the girl's force is moving leaves. She is doing work. But now look at the boy next door cleaning his sidewalk.

A force makes the leaves move. So work is being done. But is the work being done by the boy? Or by the water? **INVESTIGATE**

LEARNING TO INVESTIGATE

Can Water Do Work?

Needed: Cardboard wheel, knitting needle or long nail, pitcher of water, empty jar

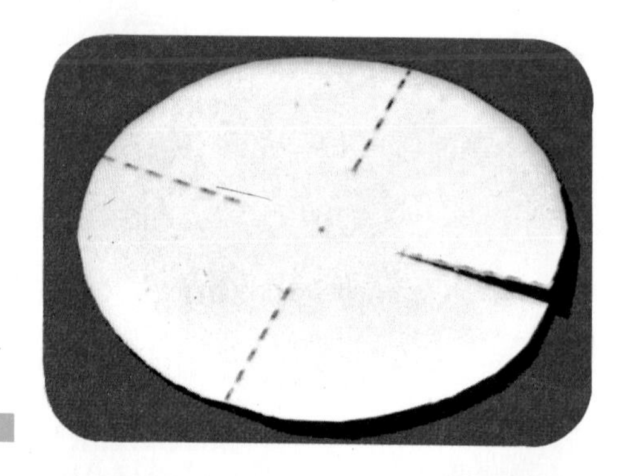

■

Cut a round piece of cardboard from a milk carton. Make cuts along the dashed lines. ■

●

Fold the edges up and down like this. ●

Push the knitting needle through the middle. You now have a wheel that can turn. Push it around with your finger. Your force makes the wheel move. You are doing work!

▲

Hold the wheel so part of it is under water. Does it turn? ▲

Now hold the wheel over the empty jar. Pour water on one edge. ◆

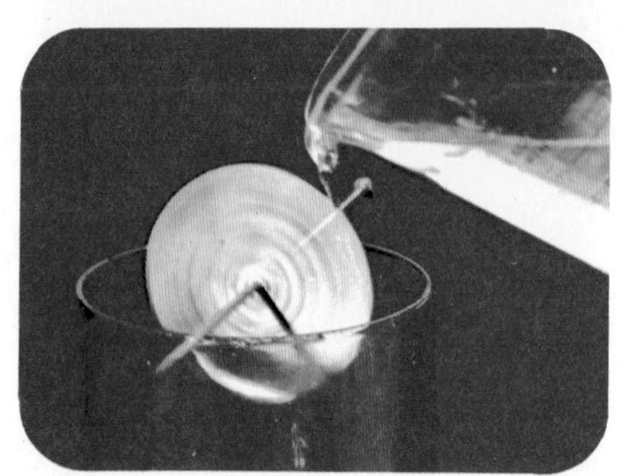

◆

Does the wheel turn? Is the water doing work?

When Water Does Work

When the water is moving it turns the little wheel. Force from the moving water makes the wheel go around. The moving water does work.

What work is moving water doing here? ■

Moving water can pull up trees, move houses, push over bridges. It can carry soil away too. Moving water can do work. When something can do work, we say it has energy. When water moves, it has energy.

In a flood, the energy of moving water destroys things. But people have thought up ways to use the energy of moving water. Let's look at one.

■

Using Energy

Here is one way to use the energy of moving water.

The water hits the top of the water wheel. The wheel turns. When this wheel was used, it turned other wheels inside the building. They ground up wheat and made it into flour.

Here is another way.

This dam is a strong wall. It holds back the water of a great river. Water is stored up behind the dam. Energy is stored in this deep, quiet water.

Here's how this stored energy is used. Gates in the dam are opened. The stored water rushes through pipes. This moving water has energy! It turns modern water wheels. They turn machines that give out electricity.

You know that electricity can do work. Electricity has energy. At this dam, the energy of moving water is changed into electric energy.

Sun Power?

Think of puddles on a sunny day. They get smaller and smaller. The water disappears! It changes to an invisible gas in the air.

The invisible gas rises. It forms a cloud in the sky. The cloud changes to rain. Water from the rain flows into a river. The river flows into a lake behind a dam.

That still water behind the dam has stored energy. What puts the energy there?

Is it the Sun? ■

Search on Your Own

Is this dog doing work? How do you know?

What kinds of work do you do? If you investigate, you could be surprised. One girl made a record that began like this:

Force Used	Things Moved	Work Done
Push	Me	Got out of bed
Pull	Door	Opened door

What will your record be like?

LOOK BACK

Is the water doing work? Explain why.

1. Waves push seaweed onto a beach.

2. Water is held back by a dam.

3. Water from a faucet cleans a dirty plate.

4. Rain beats plants down.

5. A puddle on the sidewalk is clear and still.

6. Water from a hose digs a hole in the ground.

2. Air at Work

It is a lazy summer day. The air is still. The palm trees stand straight and tall. Not a leaf is moving. No waves are on the sea.

Suddenly there is a change. The palm trees bend and sway. Their long leaves toss wildly. Waves appear. Here and there the waves have white caps of foam.

The air is no longer still. It moves. First it is a breeze. It moves faster. Now it is a wind. ■

Can a wind do work? How can something you cannot see do work? **INVESTIGATE**

■

LEARNING TO INVESTIGATE

How Can Air Do Work?

Needed: Cardboard wheel and needle or nail shown on page 86, long strip of light paper, large piece of cardboard

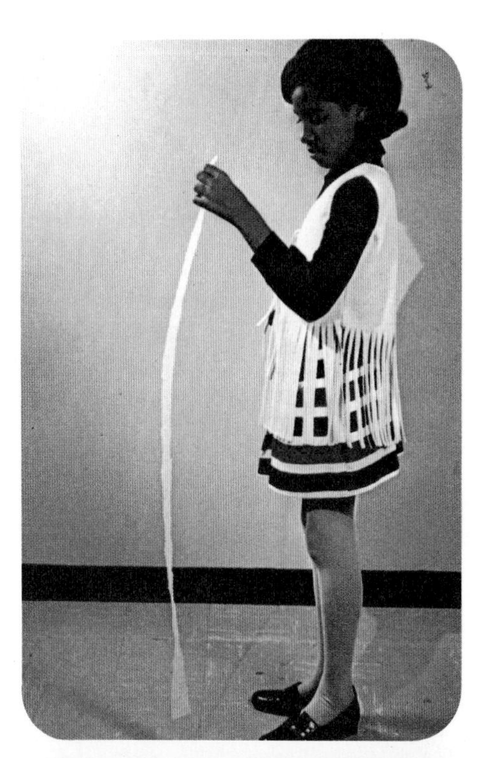

Let the strip of paper hang from your fingers. Is the air still or moving? How can you tell? ■

Ask a friend to hold the strip. Now use the cardboard as a fan. Can you make air move? Can the moving air make the strip move?

Stand where the air seems still. Does still air make the wheel go around? ●

Give the wheel a push with your finger. Can your force turn the wheel? Now take a deep breath. Can you make the wheel turn by blowing on it? ▲

Does moving air have force? What evidence do you have for your answer?

Still Air and Moving Air

You know that still water does no work. You know that moving water can do work. The same is true of air. Still air does no work. Moving air can do work.

Moving air has force. It can push. What evidence of the force of moving air do you see here?

Moving air has energy. What ways have people invented to use the energy of moving air?

Energy from the Air

Windmills were invented a long time ago. And they are still used. This one pumps water from under ground for cattle on a ranch. ●

But here is a new kind of windmill. It is being tried out in Ohio. ▲

Those big blades can be swung around and tilted to get the best results. This windmill does not pump water. It takes energy from moving air and changes it into electric energy. It may help meet our need for more energy.

●

▲

LOOK BACK

Which use the energy of moving air?

1. A white cloud moves fast across the sky.
2. A jet plane takes off.
3. A kite flies high.
4. An umbrella is blown inside out.
5. Water runs down a roof.
6. Wind pushes against a brick wall.

ON YOUR OWN

Blow up a balloon. Hold it so that the air can't escape. Now you have a balloon full of stored energy! ■

Can you find work for this stored energy to do? Can you use it to move bits of paper? Can you use it to make the balloon move? Can you use it to make a sound?

■

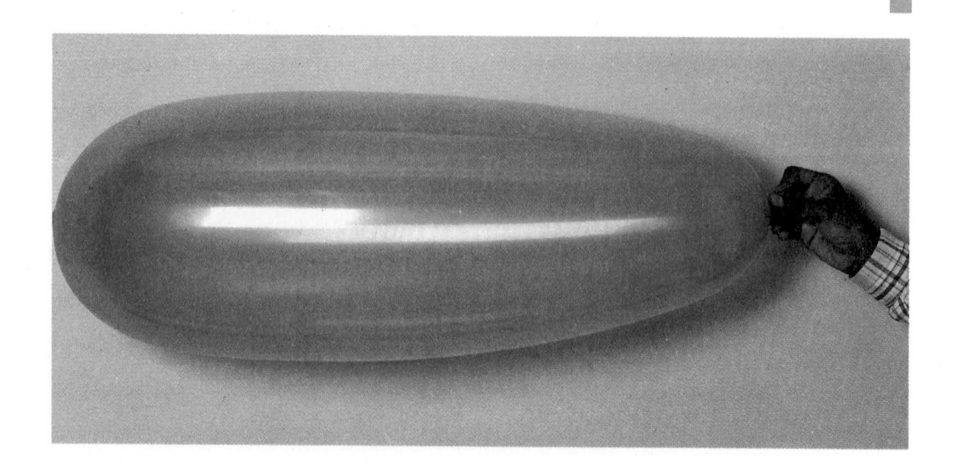

3. Electric Energy at Work

You know that inside a flashlight are dry cells. But what is inside a dry cell?

Inside the dry cell is a kind of paste. The paste is a mixture of chemicals. These chemicals have energy. A dry cell stores chemical energy.

You turn on the flashlight. This stored chemical energy changes. It changes to electric energy. The bulb lights up!

What else can this energy do? **INVESTIGATE**

Using Electric Energy

Needed: Large dry cell, large iron nail, small paper clips, length of covered wire bare at each end

Touch the nail to the clips and lift it slowly. Do clips cling to the nail? ■

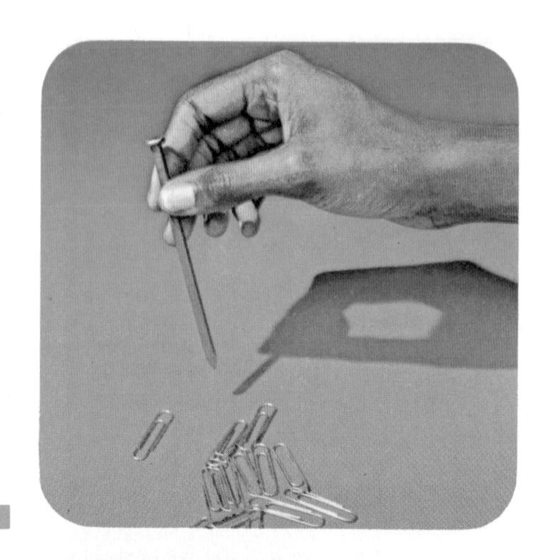

■

Wind the wire around the nail about 25 times. Fasten the bare ends to the posts on the dry cell. Now electricity flows through the wire.

Touch the nail to the clips and lift it slowly. Do clips cling to the nail? ●

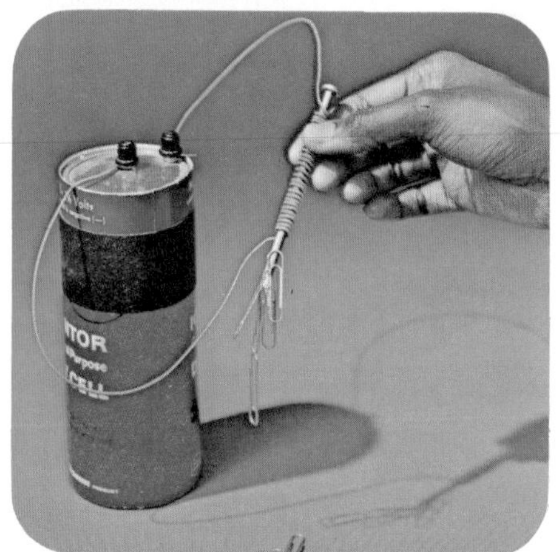

●

What do you think will happen if you unfasten one wire from the dry cell? What does happen? ▲

What is the nail like? What do you think makes it this way?

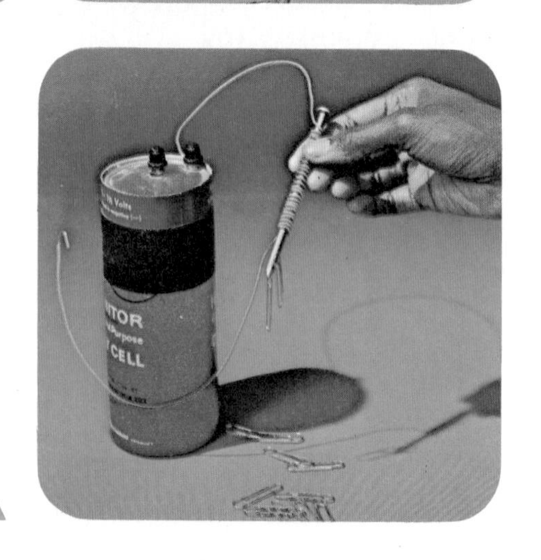

▲

Making a Magnet

What happens when you fasten the wire to the dry cell? Electricity flows out of the cell, along the wire, and back into the cell. ■

We call this flow of electricity an electric current. When the electric current flows, the nail becomes a magnet. We call it an electromagnet.

You unfasten one end of the wire. Now the electric current cannot flow. The nail stops being a magnet. Here is a magnet that can be turned on and off!

■

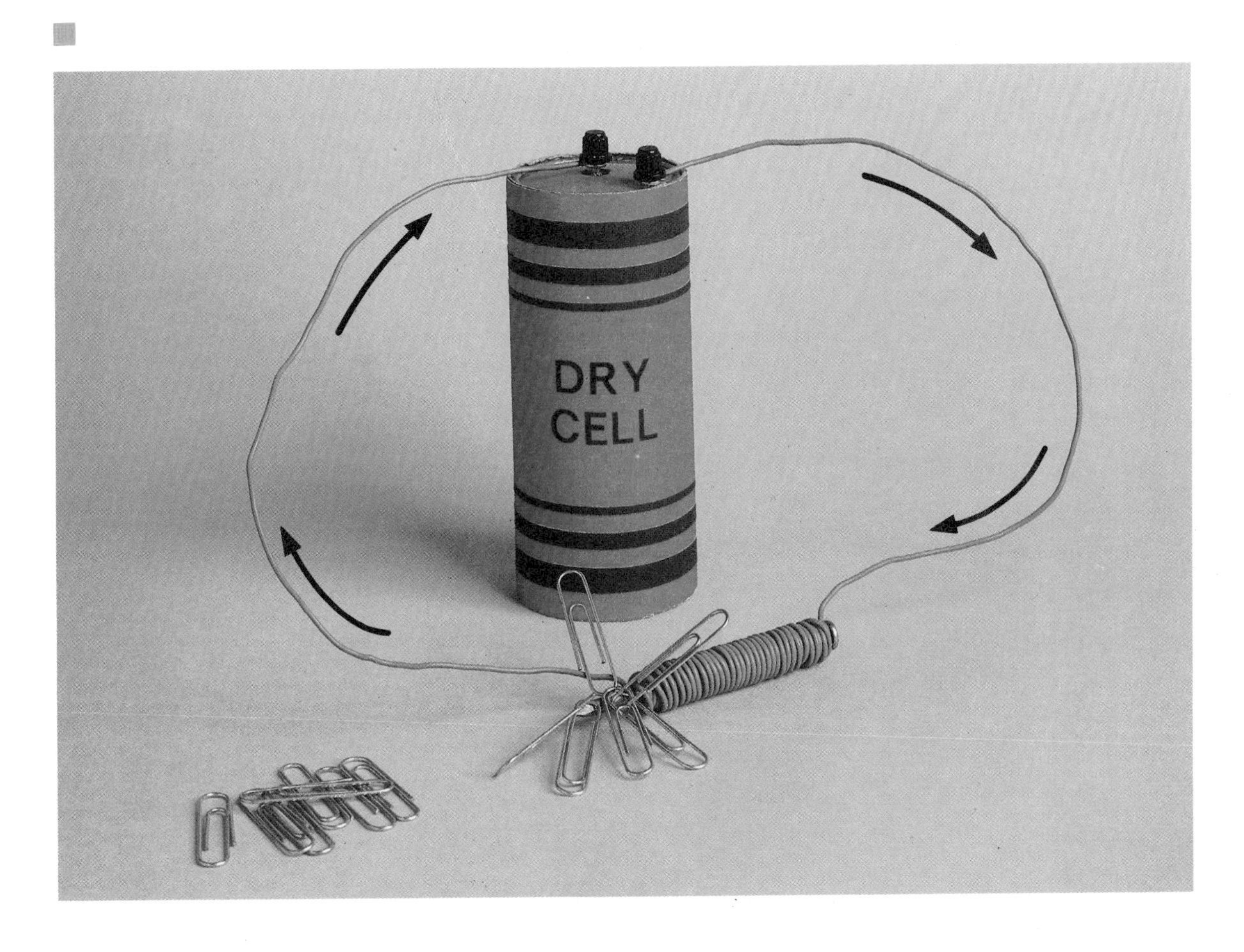

■

Using Electromagnets

You can't turn an ordinary magnet on and off. But this big electromagnet is turned on. It is holding heavy pieces of iron and steel. When it is turned off, it lets go of the load. ■

Here is the inside of an electric bell. Do you see two coils of wire? ●

The two coils are electromagnets. You turn them on by pushing a button. An electric current flows through the coils. The coils become magnets. The bell rings. You stop pushing the button. The coils stop being magnets. The bell stops ringing.

The coils of wire inside an electric motor are electromagnets also. ▲

●

▲

LOOK BACK

1. A dry cell stores
   light energy — chemical energy
2. The current that flows through a wire has
   electric energy — chemical energy
3. Electric energy can make a nail become
   a magnet — a dry cell
4. The magnet that can be turned on and off is
   an ordinary magnet — an electromagnet
5. There are electromagnets in
   dry cells — electric motors

USING WHAT YOU KNOW

Here are two pictures. How are the two things in each picture alike? How are they different?

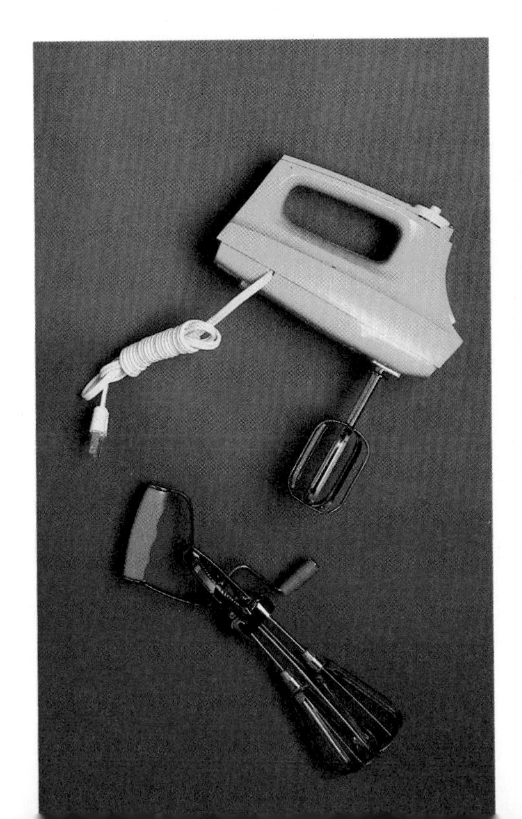

4. Fuels at Work

Cars and buses speed along. Trucks haul goods across the land. Locomotives pull trains. Ships cross oceans. Jet planes roar through the air. Rockets blast off. Energy is being used.

Food is cooked. Bread is baked. Buildings are heated and cooled. Energy is being used.

Eight candles are lit on a birthday cake! Energy is being used.

Where do we get all the energy we use?

When a Candle Burns

Where do we get energy? A candle can show us. It is made of wax, as you know. And the wick is a length of string. ●

Look what happens to the wax below the flame when the candle is lit. ▲

The wax below the flame melts. The liquid wax soaks into the wick. It climbs up in the wick. It keeps the flame burning. That liquid wax is fuel. Wax is the fuel that keeps the candle burning.

●

▲

Changing Energy

Candle wax is a fuel. It burns. It gives off light and heat. You see the light and you feel the heat.

Energy is stored in this fuel. What kind of energy do you think it is? Chemical energy is stored in candle wax.

A dry cell has chemical energy in it, you remember. The chemical energy stored in a dry cell changes to electric energy. The chemical energy in the wax changes to heat and light energy.

Where We Get Energy

Where do we get the energy for our cars and trucks? For our planes and trains? For our heaters and coolers? For all the other machines? We get energy from fuels.

Do we *make* energy when we burn a fuel? No, the energy is already there. It is stored in the fuel. We let it out. We change the stored energy to a useful kind of energy. Then we use it.

Fuels are important to us. Where do they come from? How does energy get into them? We will probe further.

LOOK BACK

1. A car and a candle both use
   light — energy
2. A candle melts its own
   wax — wick
3. Candle wax is a kind of
   fuel — energy
4. Candle wax stores
   light energy — chemical energy
5. A burning fuel is
   making energy — changing energy

USING WHAT YOU KNOW

A fuel is anything that burns and gives off heat. What fuels do you use in a day? What do you do with their energy? Make a list.

ON YOUR OWN

For some interesting ways in which fuels are used see *Energy: Its Past, Its Present, Its Future,* by Martin Gutnik, published by Children's Press, 1975. This book tells about some fuels and the use of energy.

5. Energy in Fuels

Think what happens when a log burns. ■

The wood changes, doesn't it? While it changes, it gives off two kinds of energy. You can feel one kind. You can see the other kind.

The wood has energy stored in it. When the wood burns, that stored energy changes. It changes to heat and light energy.

But how does the wood get energy in the first place?

■

Energy in Wood

A tree grows in sunlight. ■

Energy from the Sun helps the tree grow. As the tree grows, it makes wood. There is stored energy in the wood—energy from the Sun.

That energy may take years to store. But if we burn the wood, that energy changes quickly. It changes to heat and light energy. We need heat and light energy. So we use wood as a fuel.

We use another fuel that takes much longer to store up energy. Let's see why.

■

A Swamp Long Ago

It is 250 million years ago. There are no people on Earth.

Ferns are everywhere. Many of them are as tall as trees! And there are trees, too. But they look different from the trees we know.

The air is hot and damp. Splash! A giant fern falls into the water. Crash! A strange tree falls on top of it. Leaves and trees lie in the water. More leaves and more trees are falling on them.

For thousands of years plants grew in that long-ago swamp. Plants died. Plants fell in the water.

Sand and mud covered them. More plants fell. More sand and mud covered them. Layer piled on layer as time went by.

Water flowed in and made a lake. Water and sand and mud pressed down on the buried layers.

Over thousands of years the buried layers changed. The sand and mud changed to rock. The layers of plants changed to coal. ■

How Do We Know?

How can we know anything about what happened millions of years ago?

Coal is found between layers of rock. In some of the rock layers there are fossils. The fossils are prints made by plants and animals that lived long ago. The fish that left this print in rock lived millions of years ago.

Coal may have fossils in it, too. Fossils have helped scientists figure out what the Earth was like long ago.

Energy in Coal

A lump of coal is really a lump of stored energy, isn't it?

Where did the stored energy come from? About 250 million years ago some green plants took in energy from the Sun. The plants grew. They died. They were covered over. As millions of years went by, the plants were slowly changed to coal. For millions of years more, the coal stored its energy—energy from the Sun.

It takes about an hour to burn these lumps of coal. ■

■

LOOK BACK

1. A tree uses energy from
   fuels　　　　the Sun

2. Wood stores energy from
   fuels　　　　the Sun

3. Coal is made from buried layers of
   green plants　　　　sand and rock

4. Fossils are found in
   green plants　　　　rock and coal

5. We know about life long ago from
   stored energy　　　　fossils

ON YOUR OWN

Make a print for yourself. Fill a box or a tray with sand. Make the sand damp. Smooth it. Then press a small branch into the sand, carefully. Lift the branch out carefully. What's left in the sand? Try a small bone. What else might you try?

6. Oil and Gas

We burn gasoline to run cars. We burn diesel oil to run trucks and buses. We burn fuel oil to heat buildings, produce electricity, and run machines. We burn wax in candles.

Gasoline. Diesel oil. Fuel oil. Candle wax. They all come from a thick brown liquid, called petroleum. ■

■

Where does petroleum come from? It comes from rocks, under the ground. It used to be called rock oil. But how did petroleum get there?

Scientists think that petroleum started this way. Tiny plants and animals lived in the sea long, long ago. When they died, they sank to the bottom. They piled up there.

As time passed, these dead plants and animals were covered by layers of sand, mud, and shells.

Millions of years went by. The layers changed. They changed to layers of rock.

The dead plants and animals changed too. They changed to tiny drops of petroleum and tiny bubbles of natural gas, inside layers of rock.

Petroleum and natural gas come from the remains of tiny living things of long ago. This is a theory that scientists have made up. A theory is an explanation. But it has to fit the facts. This theory seems to fit the facts scientists have about petroleum and natural gas. ■

Suppose scientists discover some new facts? Suppose the theory does not fit the new facts? Then the theory will have to be changed.

Petroleum is found in rock. But isn't rock hard and solid? How can there be oil in a rock? **INVESTIGATE**

■

LEARNING TO INVESTIGATE

Can a Rock Hold Oil?

Needed: A piece of dry sandstone rock, a glass, oil, paper towels, a magnifying glass

Put three large drops of oil on the sandstone. Put three large drops on the glass. ■

Does the oil seem to sink into the sandstone? Does it seem to sink into the glass? ●

Take a paper towel. Can you wipe the oil off the glass? Off the sandstone? ▲

How do you explain what happens to the oil?

Look at the sandstone through the magnifying glass. Look at the glass. Which one seems smooth? Which seems made of tiny bits?

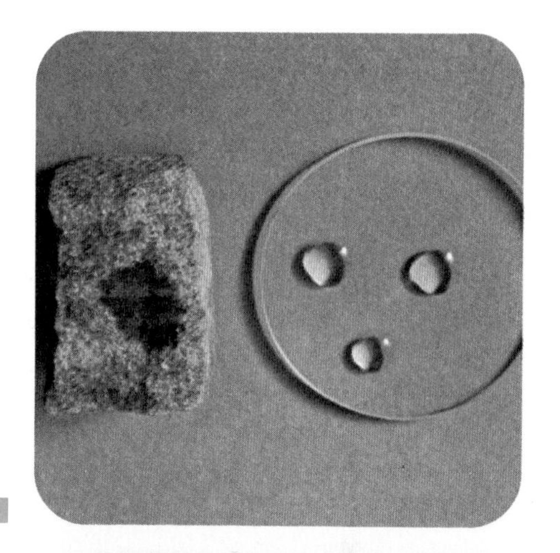

■

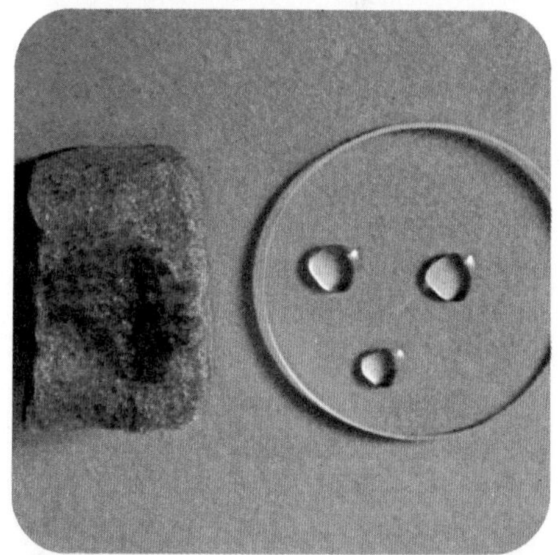

●

▲

Oil in Rock

What happens to drops of oil on a piece of sandstone rock? The oil goes right inside the rock. Sandstone is made of grains of sand. But between the grains are empty spaces! The oil goes into those spaces. ■

This is why some rocks can hold petroleum or gas. Other rocks, like marble, can't. They don't have the spaces for it.

Petroleum and natural gas have stored energy. It is really energy that came from sunlight. The sunlight fell on the Earth millions of years ago.

■

LOOK BACK

1. Petroleum is found in
   wood — rocks
2. A fuel we get from petroleum is
   coal — gasoline
3. Petroleum probably began with dead plants and animals
   on the land — in the sea
4. A theory is
   an explanation — a new fact
5. Tiny spaces that can hold oil and gas are in
   some rocks — all rocks
6. Stored energy in petroleum and gas comes from
   fuel oil — sunlight

USING WHAT YOU KNOW

Make a class mural that shows how coal was formed, and how it is used.

ON YOUR OWN

Find out something about how we get petroleum and gas out of the ground. And how we discover where they are, to begin with.

7. Energy from the Sun

This is a radiometer. ■

Inside the glass bulb is a kind of wheel. Now the wheel is spinning around. ●

What makes the radiometer go? There is a clue in the pictures.

In the shade, the wheel does not turn. But in the sunlight, the wheel spins. Sunlight makes the radiometer go.

You know the Sun gives off energy. We call energy from the Sun solar energy. It is solar energy that makes the radiometer wheel spin.

■

●

▲

We have other uses for solar energy. It can dry clothes hung on a line, for instance.

When farmers plant a crop, they are putting solar energy to work. Green wheat plants use solar energy to make their food. They make food for us, too, when the wheat is ripe. ▲

Can you think of another use for solar energy?

Now we are planning new ways to use solar energy. Let's look at some.

This home is heated by a furnace, like many homes. But it is also heated by solar energy.

On the roof are solar energy collectors. When sunlight hits the collectors, they get hot. They turn the solar energy into heat. This heat is used to warm the house. Heat from the furnace may be used too, when it is needed.

You may wonder what happens when the Sun is behind clouds. What happens at night, when no solar energy reaches the collectors? The answer is: heat can be *stored!*

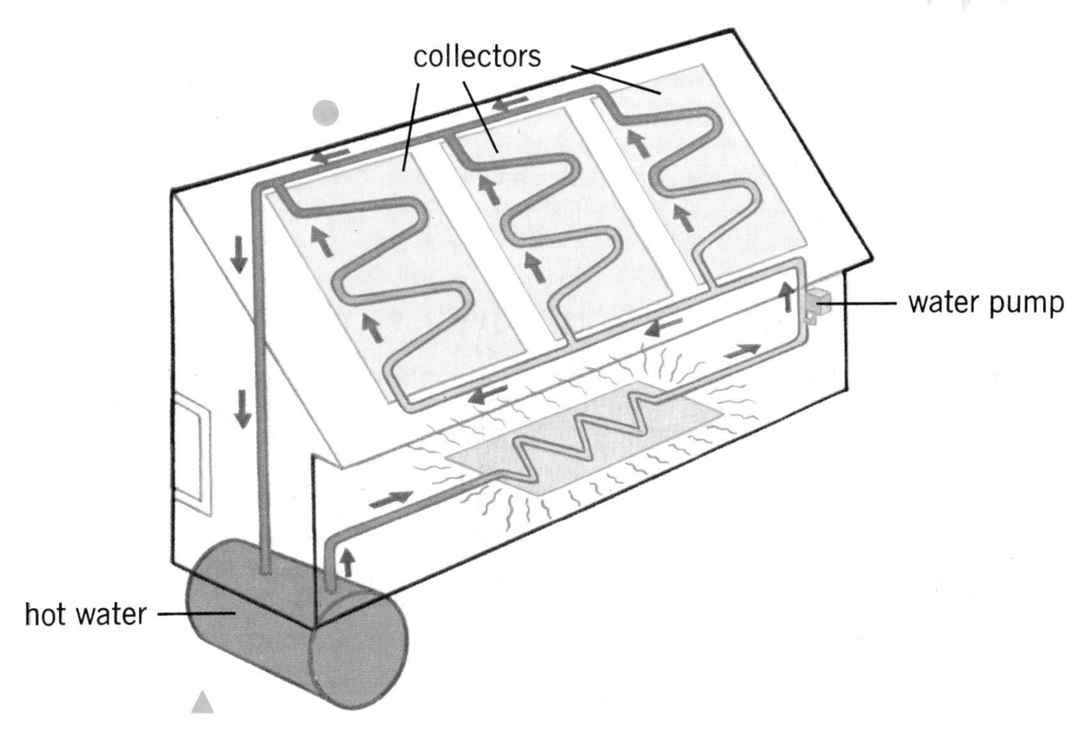

Sunlight hits the collectors. The collectors turn the solar energy into heat. The heat warms water inside the collectors. ●

This hot water is sent down to a large tank. The hot water is stored in the tank. In this way, heat is stored in the tank. ▲

What happens at night or when the Sun is behind clouds? The water in the tank can be used to warm the house. It can add to heat from the furnace, if the furnace is used. Either way, fuel is saved.

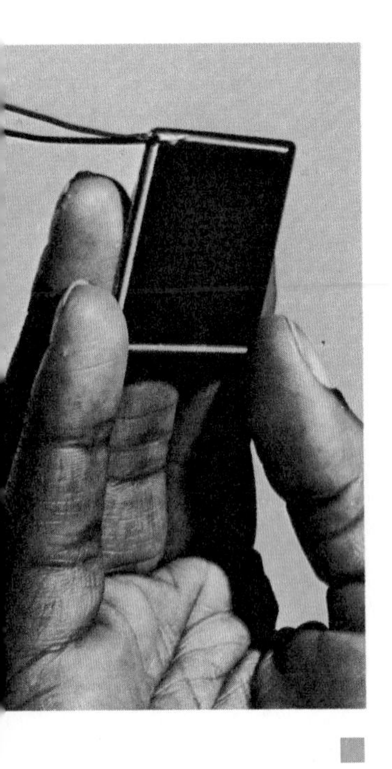

Here is another way we use solar energy. This is a solar cell. ■

When sunlight hits the solar cell, the cell changes the solar energy to electric energy. A solar cell is expensive. But it can do some special jobs very well.

Have you ever seen a TV program "by satellite"? The satellite is out in space. It receives the program and sends it out again. Thus the program is sent around the world. ●

■

The satellite uses electric energy to do this. It gets the electric energy from its solar cells.

●

LOOK BACK

1. A radiometer wheel turns by
   solar energy   electric energy

2. Green plants use
   solar energy   electric energy

3. Collectors change solar energy into
   heat   water

4. A water tank can store
   light   heat

5. A solar cell turns light into
   heat   electric energy

USING WHAT YOU KNOW

Look in magazines and newspapers for pictures of solar energy being put to use. If you keep a Science Searchbook, you can put the pictures in it.

ON YOUR OWN

Can a magnifying glass be used as a solar energy collector?

Wheels turn. Motors hum. Forces make things move. Work is being done. Energy is being used.

We use the energy of moving air and moving water. We use chemical energy and electric energy. We use heat and light energy. We use solar energy. And we change energy from one form to another.

We use energy in fuels. Wood. Coal. Gas. Petroleum. When a fuel burns, its stored energy changes to energy we can use.

Scientists think petroleum was made long ago from the remains of tiny plants and animals. If this theory is true, then we know where the energy in our fuels came from. It came from the Sun.

Energy can be changed from one form to another.

Explain where the energy comes from.

1. A windmill is pumping water. ■
2. A girl is riding her bicycle.
3. A car is going up a hill.
4. A candle is lighting the room.
5. Soup is cooking on a gas range.
6. A flashlight is turned on. ●
7. A house is broken apart by flood waters.

■

●

Answer these questions.

▲

8. How do green plants get to be black coal? ▲
9. We burn wood to get its energy. How does wood get energy?
10. What theory do scientists have about how petroleum was made?

5/Earth in Space

Would you like living in space?

These astronauts lived for weeks in this big spacecraft, Skylab. They did investigations. They observed what happened. They found out much about space and living in space.

They worked hard. They played hard, too. They exercised, played games, read books, listened to music.

But you *are* living in space. You are living on planet Earth. It is speeding through space, right now, as you read this.

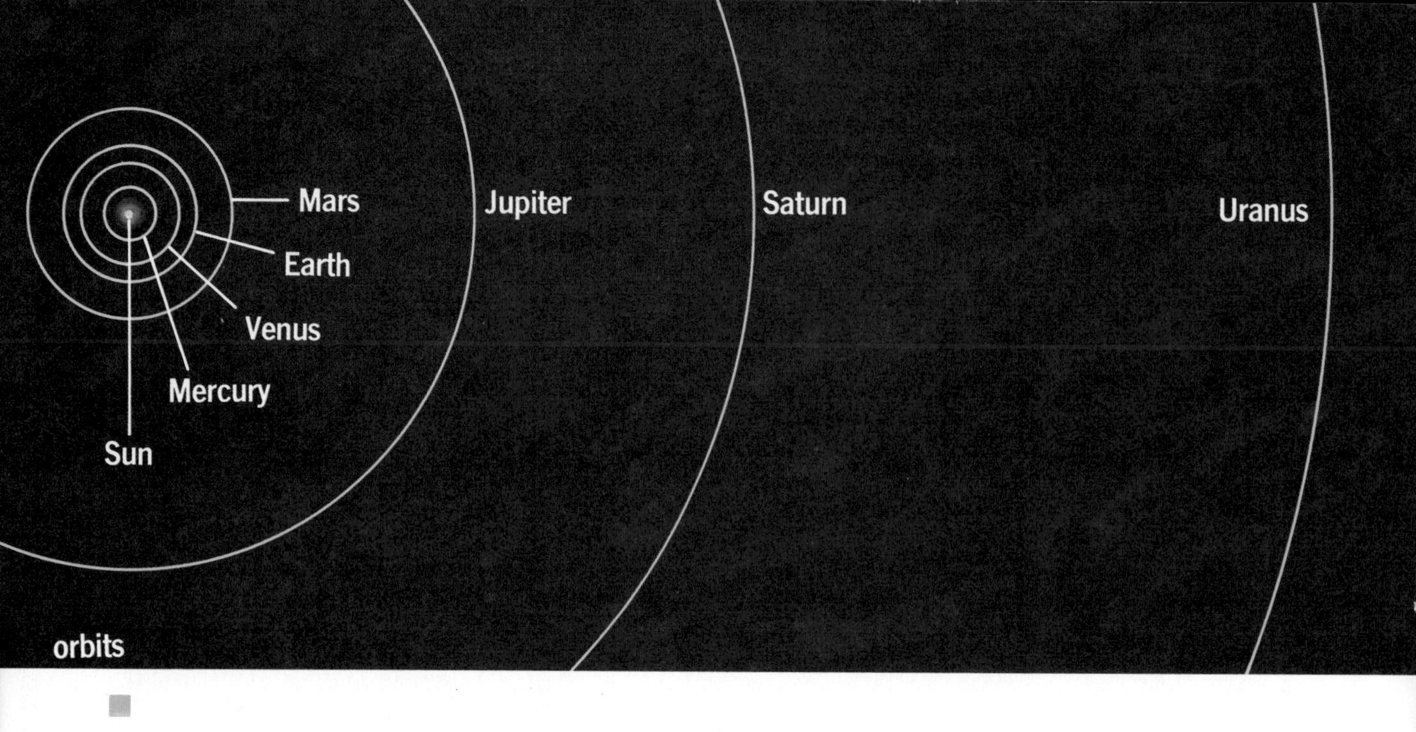

1. Too Much or Too Little

Planet Earth is your home. It travels around the Sun, as you know. But it's not alone. Eight other planets travel around the Sun. Each planet travels its own space path—its orbit.

Nine planets speed around the Sun! Can you find their orbits on the space map?

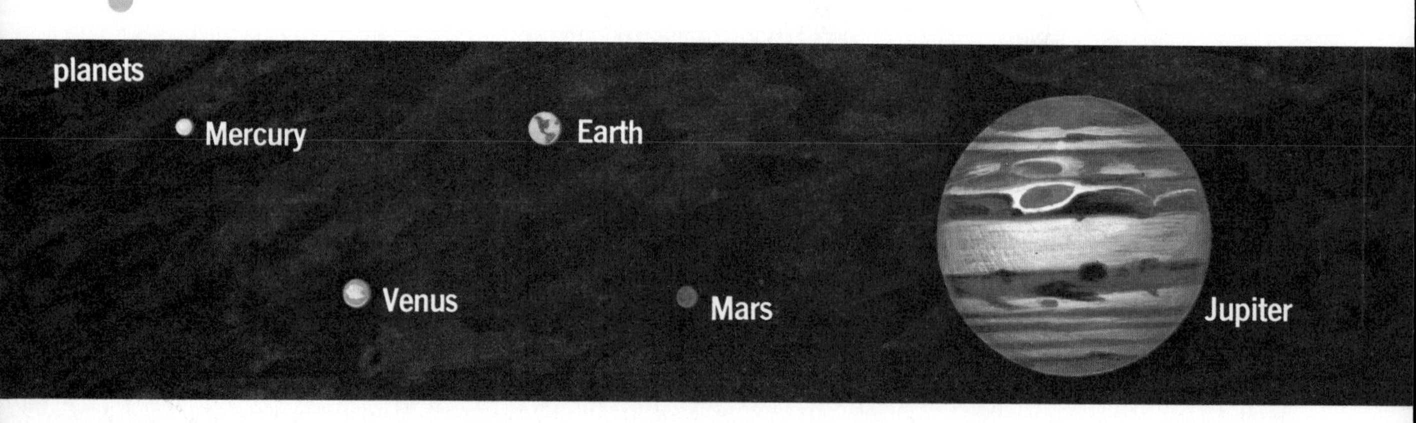

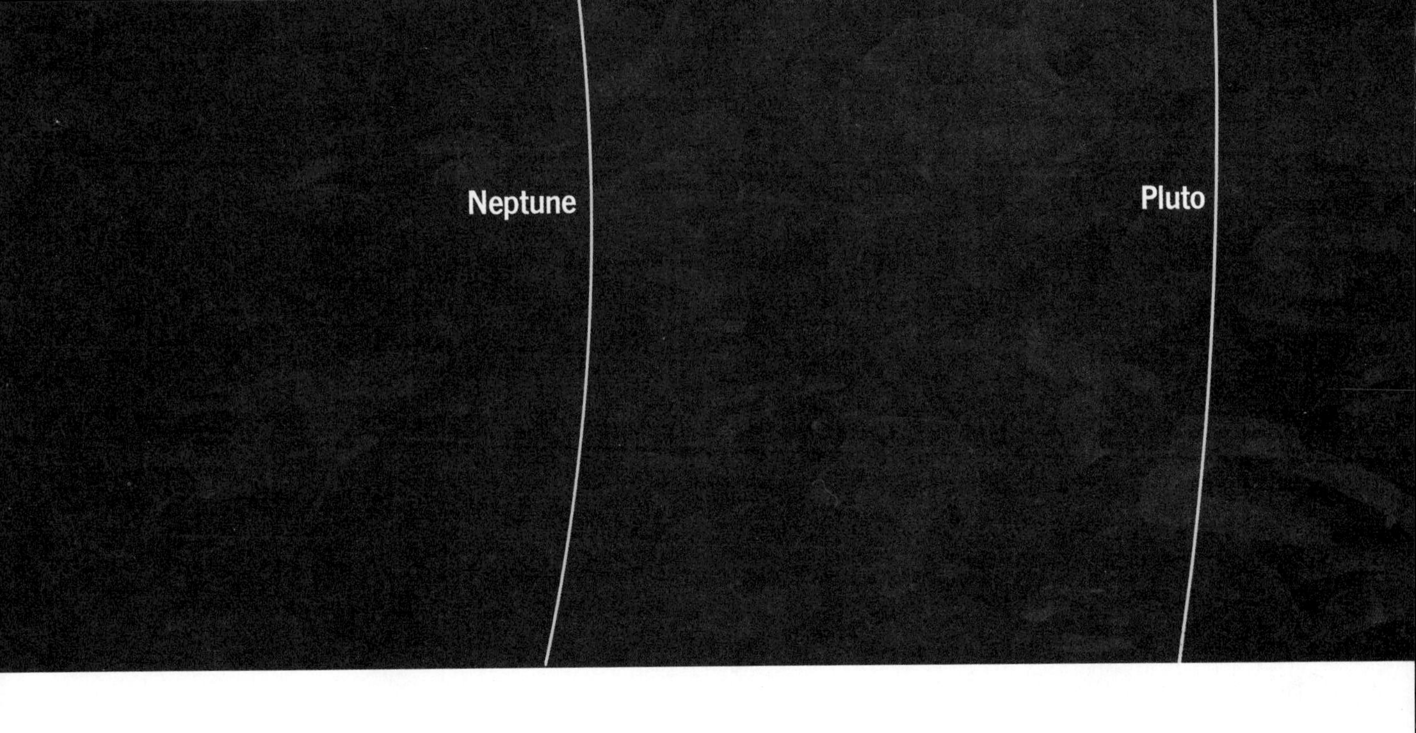

Is Earth the planet nearest the Sun? Is it the planet farthest from the Sun?

Is Earth the biggest planet? Here is how the planets compare in size. Are you surprised?

We call the Sun and its nine planets the solar system. Let's take a closer look at these parts of the solar system. Let's look at each planet.

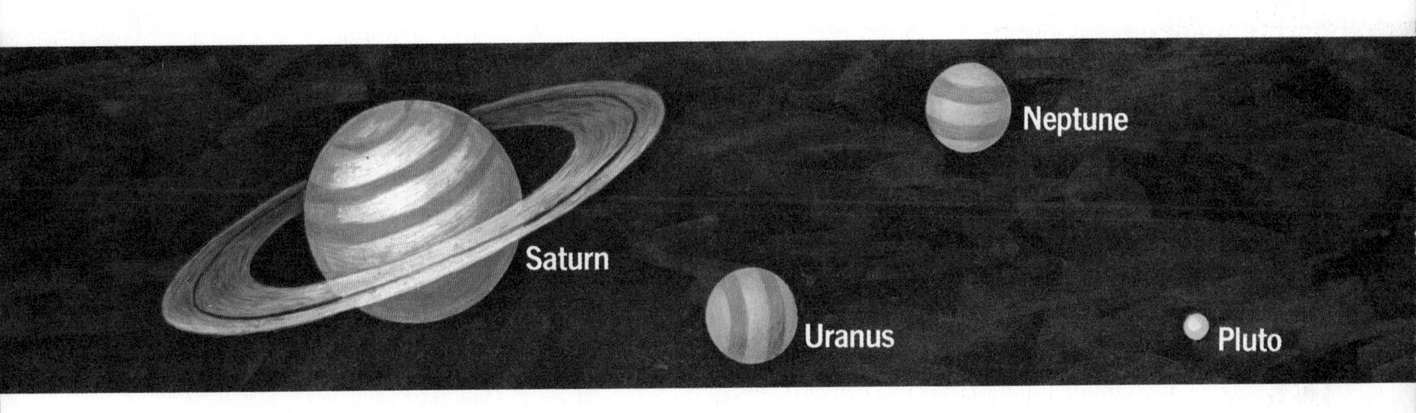

A Look at Mercury

You would need protection from great heat if you visited Mercury. Mercury is the planet nearest the Sun. The sunny side of Mercury is far hotter than the hottest day on Earth. ■

Mercury gets too much heat from the Sun. None of the plants or animals we know could live in such heat.

A Look at Pluto

If you visit Pluto, the Sun may look like this! ●

Pluto is the planet farthest from the Sun. Even in daytime it is almost dark there. And it is colder on Pluto than it ever gets on Earth.

Pluto gets too little heat and light from the Sun. Nothing we know about could live on Pluto.

A Look at Another Planet

The first planet you looked at was too hot. The next one was too cold. Look at another planet.

From space you see that this planet has land and water. Snow and ice are in some places. Other places look very warm.

You see clouds around the planet. Your space ship shoots into a layer of air. You fly over the surface of the planet.

You come still closer to the surface. This planet is different!

There are living things in the air. There are living things in the water. The land is green with living things. On the land living things crawl, hop, walk, run.

There are *people* on this planet. They work and play, with hands and brains. They think and learn. They talk. They write. They make music. They make pictures. They play games. They do amazing things.

Of course you know this planet. It is your planet, Earth.

Earth is not too near the Sun. It is not too far from it. To us, planet Earth is just about the right distance from the Sun.

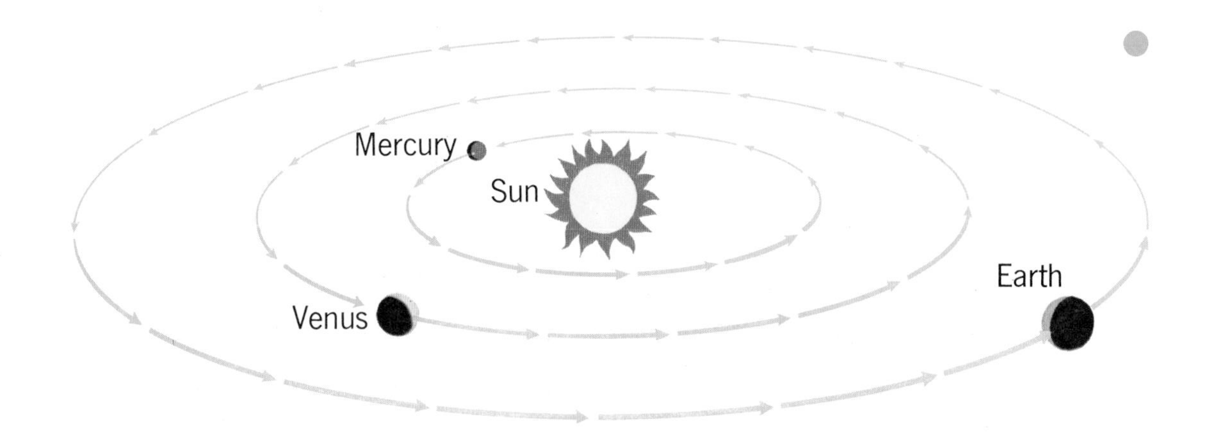

LOOK BACK

1. Each planet has its own
   Sun orbit
2. Planets in our solar system travel around
   the Earth the Sun
3. Our solar system has
   eight planets nine planets
4. The planet nearest the Sun is
   Pluto Mercury
5. A planet that gets little light and heat is
   Pluto Mercury
6. To see living things, visit the planet
   Mercury Earth

ON YOUR OWN

The space map and pictures on pages 130 and 131 will help you answer these questions.

1. Which planet makes the longest trip?
2. Which planet's orbit is nearest Earth?
3. Which is the smallest planet?
4. Which is the largest planet?
5. Which planet is farthest from Earth?

2. On Planet Earth

There are places on Earth that are cold all the time. ■

There are places that are warm all the time. ●

And there are places that are warm some of the time, and cold some of the time!

Yet the whole Earth gets energy from the Sun. Why is one part always cold? Why is another part always warm?

■

●

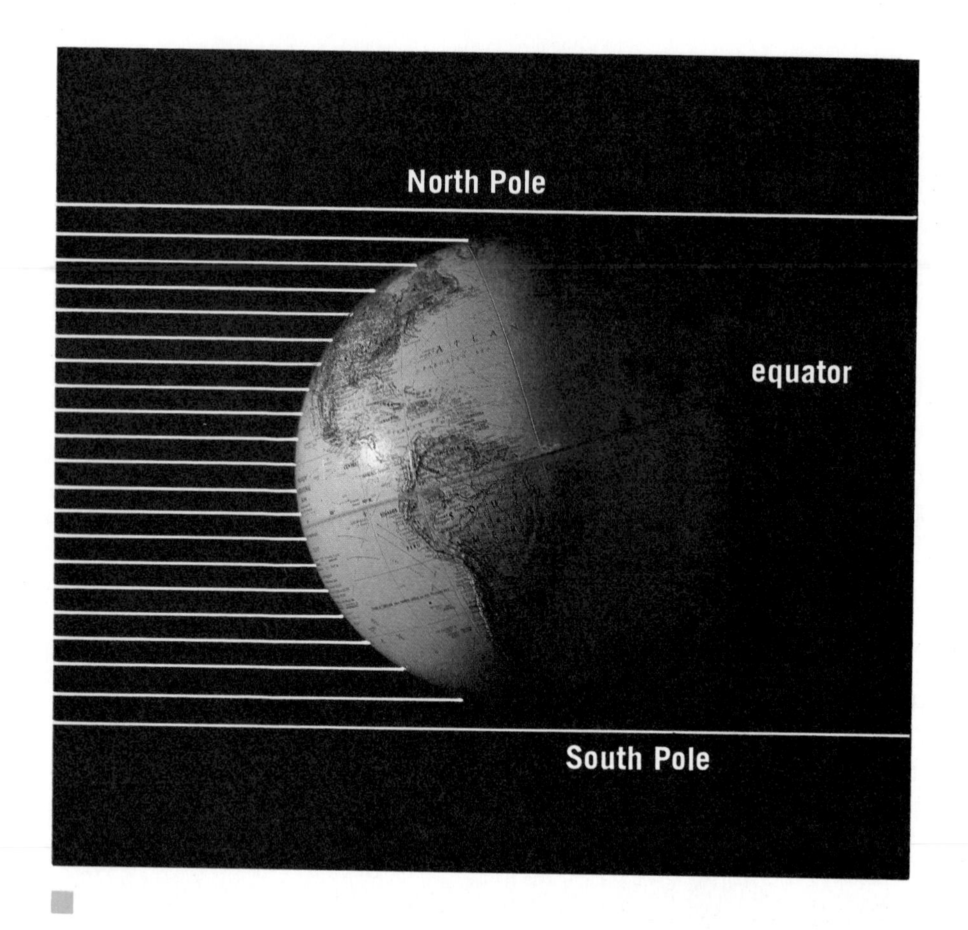

It is cold all the time at the North Pole. But at the equator it is warm all the time.

Look how the rays of sunlight hit the Earth at the equator. Here the Earth gets plenty of solar energy. It is warm here.

But look what happens at the North Pole. Here the rays hit the Earth at a slant. The solar energy is spread thin over this part of the Earth. That's why it is cold here.

Solar energy that hits the Earth turns to heat. The Earth *traps* this heat. INVESTIGATE

LEARNING TO INVESTIGATE

How Can Heat Be Trapped?

Needed: Two thermometers, a coat hanger, a plastic bag, string, sunlight

Hang the thermometers on the coat hanger. ■

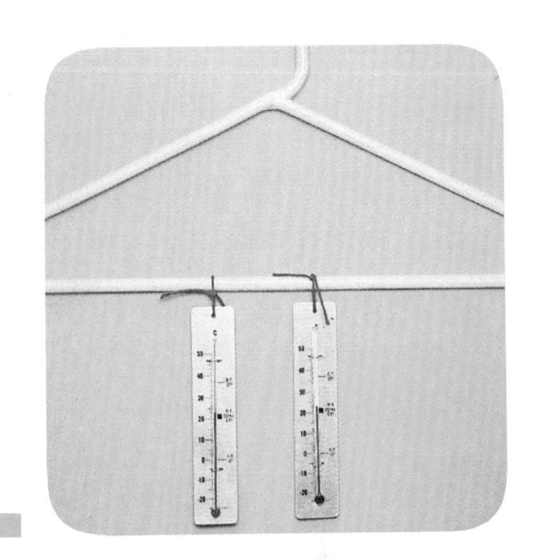

■

Put the hanger where sunlight hits the thermometers. Wait until they reach the same temperature.

Now open the plastic bag so that it fills with air. Put it around one of the thermometers. Make sure that there is plenty of air around the thermometer. Then tie the bag shut with a piece of string. ●

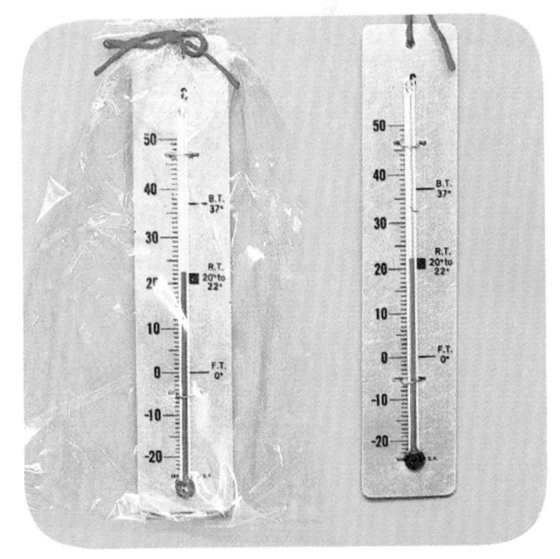

●

Keep the thermometers in the sunlight. Does one get warmer than the other? ▲

How do you explain what happens?

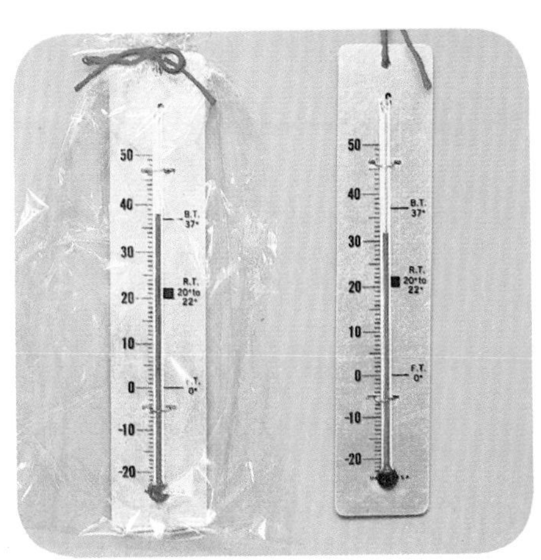

▲

A Heat Trap

Both thermometers are warmed by sunlight in the investigation. But one thermometer gets warmer than the other. The one that gets warmer has the plastic bag around it.

What does the plastic bag do? It keeps a layer of air around that thermometer. The air can't move away. It becomes warmer and warmer. Heat is trapped in that air.

There is a layer of air around the Earth, you know. That air traps heat. When sunlight warms the Earth, the Earth's air is warmed too. Heat trapped in the air warms the Earth.

One half of the Earth is always in sunlight. The other half is always in shadow.

But the Earth turns. We move from sunlight to shadow, from day to night. We move from shadow to sunlight, from night to day.

At night the part of the Earth not getting sunlight cools off. A little of the Earth's heat leaks away. It goes into space. But most of the Earth's heat is kept from leaving. The layer of air around the Earth holds the heat.

That air traps heat. If it did not, Earth would be a very cold place.

Search on Your Own

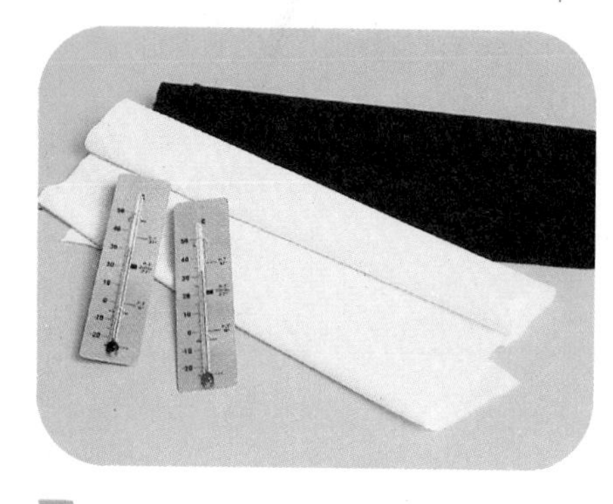

Some people like to wear white clothes on hot, sunny days. They say that white clothes are cooler than black. Are they right?

Plan an investigation with black and white cloth. Find out which is cooler in sunlight.

LOOK BACK

1. Solar energy that hits the Earth becomes
   light heat
2. Solar energy is spread thin at
   the North Pole the equator
3. The Earth's air traps
   light heat
4. The half of the Earth in shadow at night
   cools off heats up
5. Without air the Earth would be
   colder at night warmer at night
6. Some of the Earth's heat goes into
   orbit space

3. Exploring a Planet

It is about 15 minutes before sunset in this desert. ■

By the look of it, this desert might be in Mexico. Or California. But it is on Mars.

We sent out two spacecraft in 1976. We called them Vikings. Each Viking traveled for months through space. Each landed safely on Mars.

Each Viking took pictures. It observed the weather. It tested the soil near it. And it looked for signs of life on Mars.

■

A Viking spacecraft carries no astronauts. It is a machine for exploring.

But people on Earth made that machine. They steered it to Mars, by radio, and told it what to do when it landed. The Viking sent back information to them, by radio and television.

For example, the Viking received orders to test the soil on Mars. It stuck out a small shovel. It scooped up a little soil. Then it tested the soil for signs of living things.

The Vikings scooped up no living things. But to know for certain about life on Mars, scientists need more evidence.

That red color of land on Mars may come from iron. We have iron on Earth, don't we? There was once water on Mars, more water than we thought. The land shows signs of old streams. And it shows signs of rushing winds.

We have walked on the Moon. Now we are reaching out far beyond the Moon. Our spacecraft explore the solar system. One day we will walk on Mars.

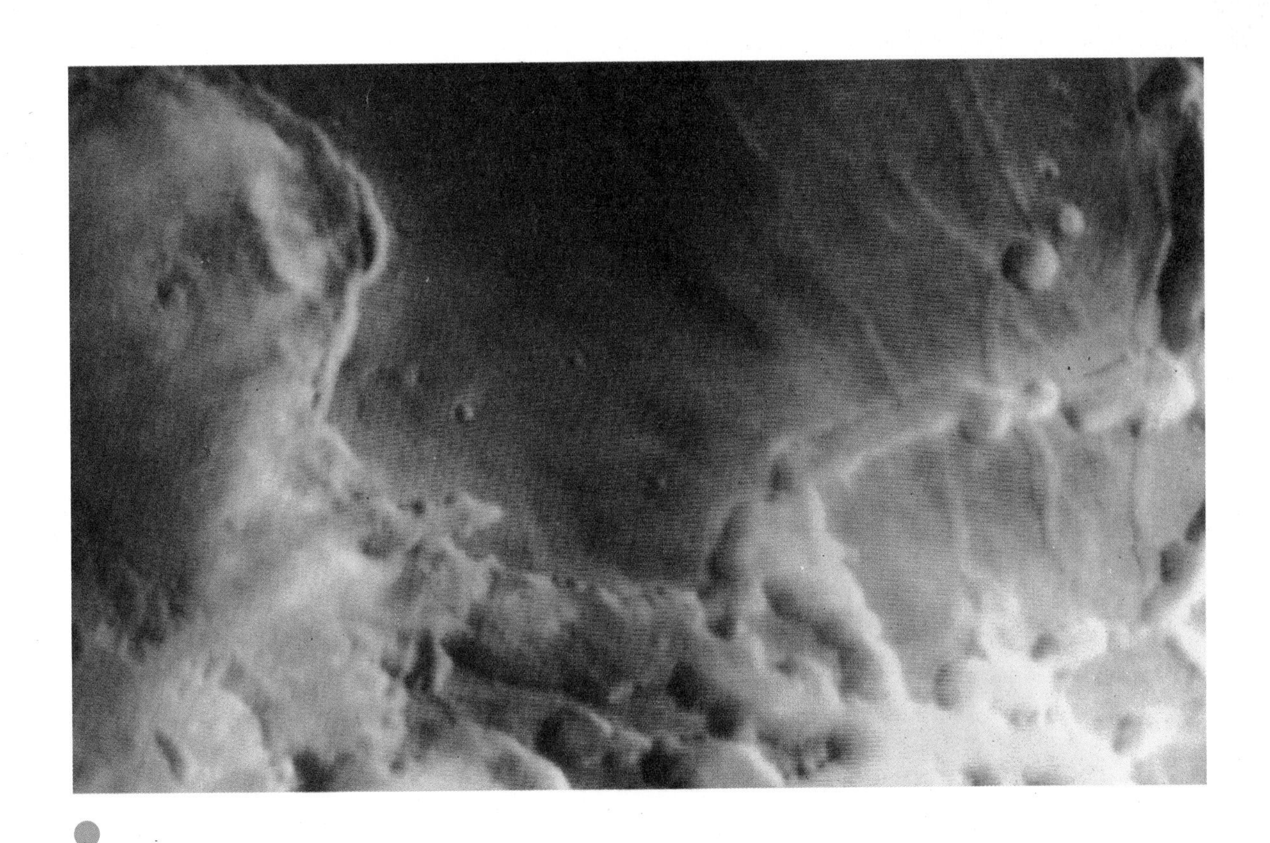

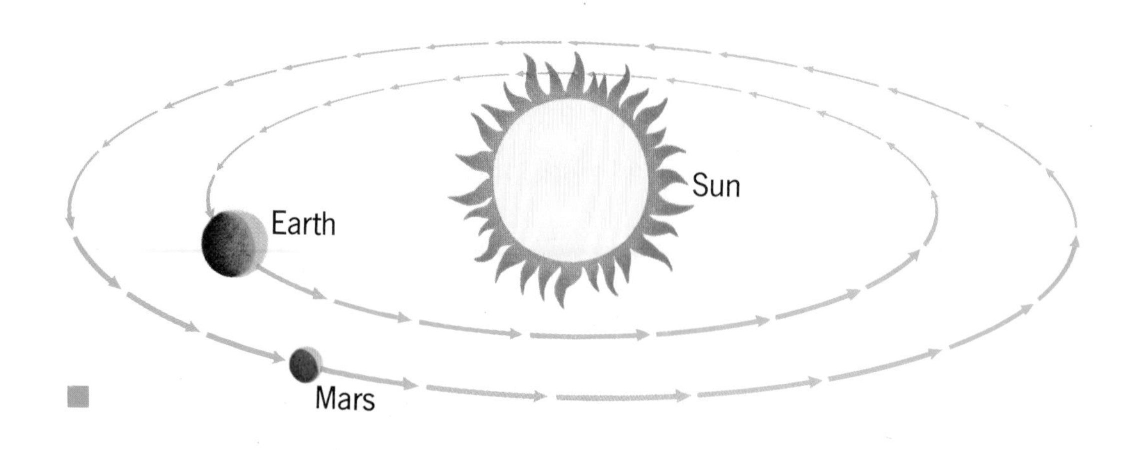

Mars and Earth

Mars is two hundred times farther away from Earth than the Moon. Mars is only half as big as the Earth.

The air on Mars is different from the air on Earth. And the air on Mars is thinner. It traps less heat from the Sun. So Mars' nights are colder than the coldest night on Earth. Mars cools off fast at night.

Are you wondering what a warm day is like on Mars? It may become about as warm as a spring day here on Earth.

Day and night on Mars are about as long as they are on Earth. But a year on Mars has about 700 days! It takes Mars almost two of our years to make one trip around the Sun. ■ See for yourself what it's like. INVESTIGATE

LEARNING TO INVESTIGATE

Earth and Mars Around the Sun

Needed: Signs for *Earth, Sun,* and *Mars,* meter stick, chalk and two friends to help

You be the Sun. Ask one friend to be the Earth. Ask the other friend to be Mars.

Have Earth stand 4 meters from the Sun. Have Mars stand 6 meters from the Sun. ■

Earth and Mars are to move around the Sun in their orbits. When you say "Go!", they start walking around the Sun. Mars should take twice as long as Earth to go once around the Sun.

How can you do this?

■

Alike and Different

Mars is the planet most like planet Earth.

Day and night on Mars are about as long as on Earth. Both planets have water frozen in the ground. Both have snow and ice. Both have air. Both get energy from the Sun.

Mars and Earth are also different. Mars is about half as big as Earth. It takes about twice as long to travel around the Sun. Mars gets less energy from the Sun than Earth gets.

Mars has two very small moons. A Viking took this photo of one. ■

So far we have not found life on Mars.

■

LOOK BACK

1. The Vikings that traveled to Mars were
   astronauts | spacecraft
2. On Mars the Vikings found no signs of
   water | life
3. Soil on Mars is red from
   uranium | iron
4. Nights on Mars are
   very cold | very warm
5. Mars is the planet
   least like Earth | most like Earth

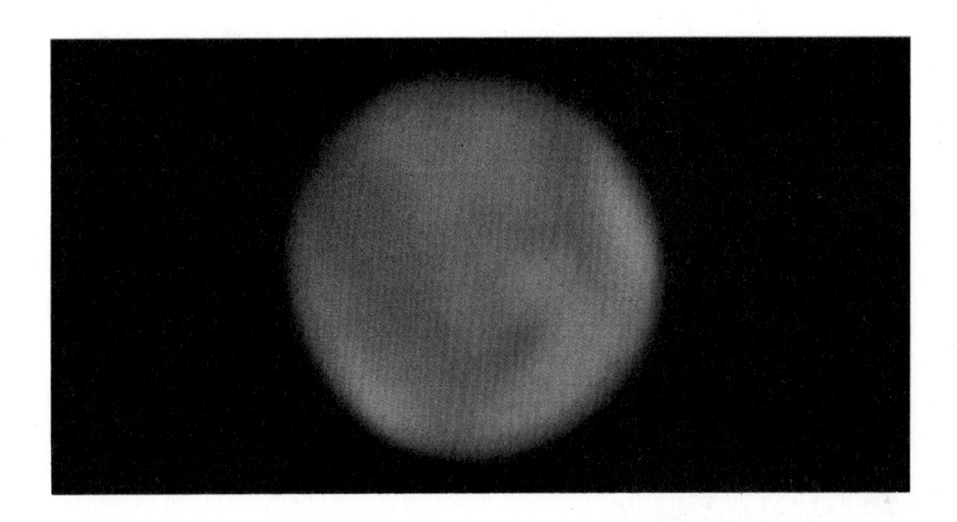

ON YOUR OWN

Look for books about the solar system when you go to the library. Here is one you may like: *The Solar System*, by Isaac Asimov, published by Follett, 1975. This book tells you about the nine planets and explores the mysteries of space.

4. Mercury and the Other Planets

Mercury is the smallest planet. It is about the size of our Moon. This photo of Mercury was taken by a spacecraft. ■

Mercury is the planet closest to the Sun. Its days are very hot. But its nights are very cold, because Mercury has almost no air. Air can trap heat, remember. The air on Mercury traps almost no heat.

While we are having 59 days and nights on Earth, Mercury is having one long day and night. But Mercury speeds around the Sun in only 88 days.

■

▲

●

Venus

Have you seen the "evening star" shining brightly? It's not a star. It's the planet Venus.

Next to the Sun and Moon, Venus is the brightest light we see in the sky. Its orbit is nearest to Earth's orbit. And Venus is about the same size as Earth. But Venus is much hotter than Earth. Can you think why?

Through a telescope this is all we can see of Venus from Earth. ● But spacecraft have flown to Venus and photographed it. ▲

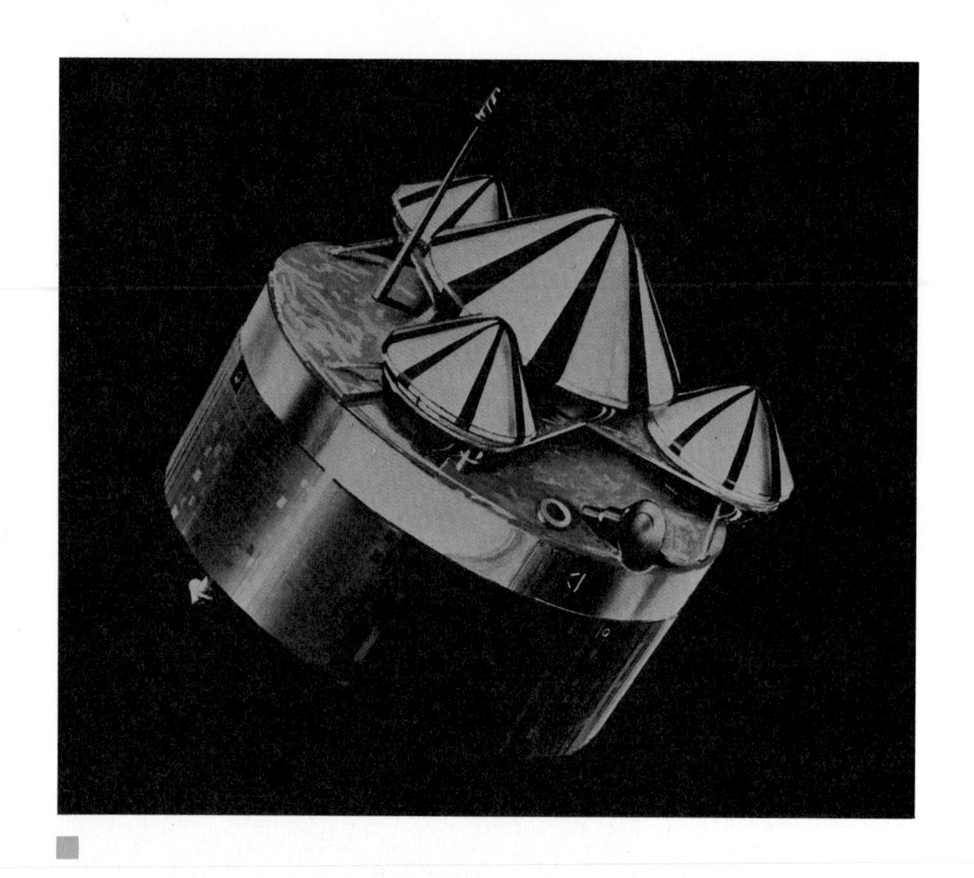

Spacecraft have landed on Venus.

The spacecraft carried no astronauts. It carried instruments only. It sent information about Venus back to Earth by radio.

Now we know how long a day and night is on Venus. It is as long as 243 of our days and nights. The air on Venus is mostly carbon dioxide gas. There is very little oxygen.

Spacecraft took the temperature on Venus. It was much hotter than boiling water. Venus is far too hot for the kinds of plants and animals we know.

Jupiter

As a spacecraft flew near, it took this photo of planet Jupiter.

Jupiter is the biggest planet in the solar system. There are no signs of oxygen or water on Jupiter. Day or night, it is very cold.

A day and night on Jupiter is only about 10 hours long. But Jupiter takes 12 years to travel once around the Sun.

Jupiter has thirteen moons.

Saturn

Saturn is the second biggest planet in the solar system. The rings around Saturn are made up of small, solid bits of matter.

Saturn has no water and no oxygen. It is farther from the Sun than Jupiter is. So its days and nights are even colder than Jupiter's.

A day and night on Saturn is only about 10 hours long. But Saturn takes about 29 years to make one trip around the Sun.

Saturn has ten moons.

Uranus, Neptune, and Pluto

Planet Uranus is far from the Sun and very cold. A day and night there is about 11 hours long. It takes about 84 years to go once around the Sun. Uranus has rings around it. And moons.

Neptune is even colder than Uranus. Its day and night is about 16 hours long. It takes about 165 years for one trip around the Sun. Like Mars, Neptune has two moons.

Pluto is farthest from the Sun. It's the coldest planet. And it takes the longest to go around the Sun, about 248 years. ●

Are there planets beyond Pluto? We don't know. Perhaps one day a spacecraft will find out.

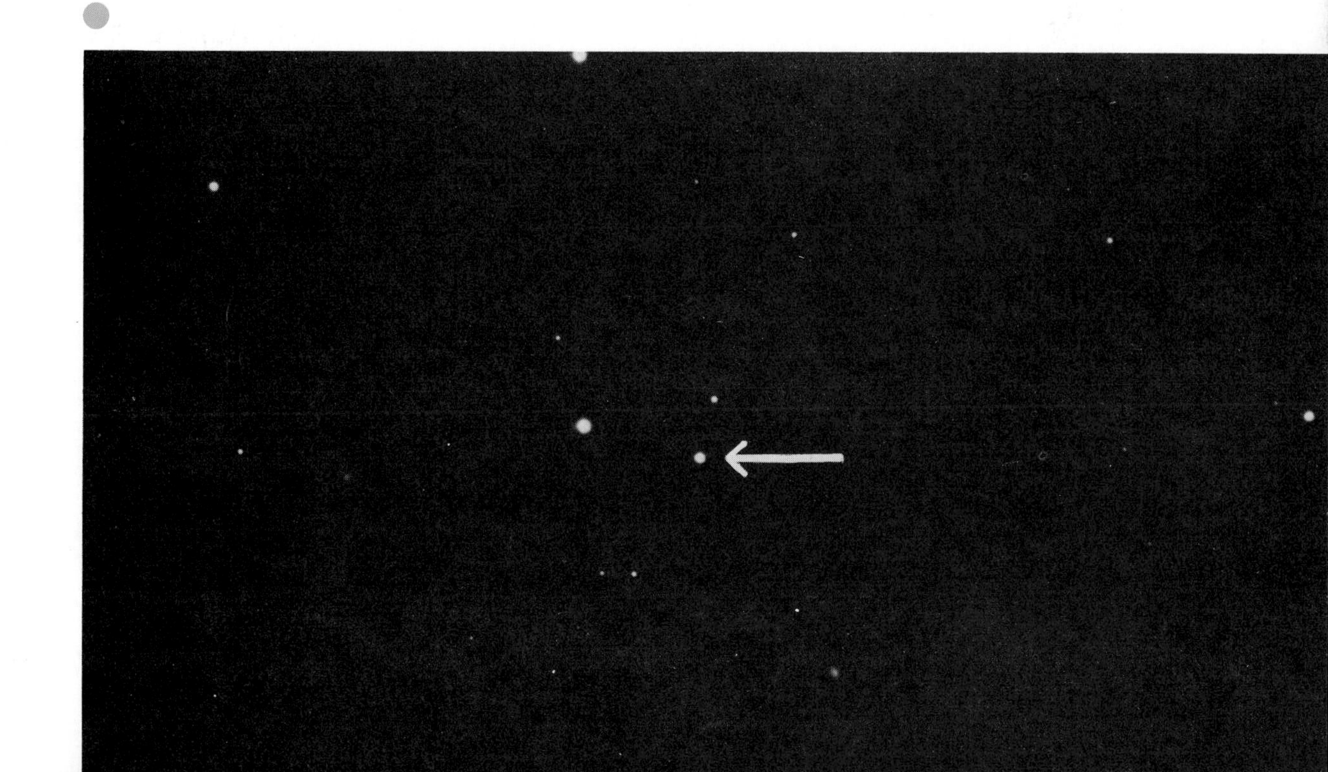

LOOK BACK

1. The smallest planet in the solar system is
   Jupiter　　Mercury

2. The planet nearest the Sun is
   Pluto　　Mercury

3. The coldest planet is
   Venus　　Pluto

4. There are rings around
   Neptune　　Saturn

5. To go around the Sun, each planet takes
   the same time　　a different time

6. The planet we know has living things is
   Earth　　Mars

ON YOUR OWN

Pick one of the nine planets. Make a study of it.

Make pictures of it, with paint or crayons. Or collect cutout pictures. Find out things like these: How have scientists studied the planet? What have they found out? Have spacecraft flown around the planet? Landed on it?

Why not make a model of the planet you choose to study? A ball of some kind might make a good starting point.

■

5. Our Nearest Neighbor

Take a good look at the Moon on a clear night. ■

The Moon is in orbit around the Earth. It makes one trip around the Earth in about 4 weeks. The Moon is Earth's satellite.

When you look at the Moon, you are looking across 400 thousand kilometers of space. But in our solar system that's not far. The Sun is 150 million kilometers away.

Where does the Moon get its light? From the Sun.

When you see the Moon at night, it is in sunlight. But you are not. You are on the dark side of the Earth.

Look at the Moon every few nights for about a month. Watch how its shape changes.

When there is a Full Moon you see all of the sunny side of the Moon. You see half the sunny side when there is a Half Moon. When you see a New Moon, you see just a thin slice of the Moon's sunny side.

Full Moon   Half Moon   New Moon   Half Moon   Full Moon

Almost 400 years ago a man named Galileo made one of the first telescopes. He decided to look at the Moon through it.

Galileo was amazed at what he saw. There were mountains and valleys on the Moon!

▲

Other scientists studied the Moon through their telescopes. They saw that the Moon always kept the same side toward the Earth. We always see this side of the Moon. ▲

How can this happen? **INVESTIGATE**

LEARNING TO INVESTIGATE

The Same Side of the Moon

Needed: Signs for *Earth, Moon,* and *Sun,* and two friends to help

You be the Moon. One friend is the Sun. The other is the Earth.

You stand near the Earth. Face the Earth. The Sun stands farther away.

Move in a circle around the Earth. Be sure you always face the Earth.

Ask your friend the Sun to watch as you go around the Earth. Ask your friend if you *turn* as you go around!

Why do we always see the same side of the Moon from the Earth?

The Other Side of the Moon

Why do we always see the same side of the Moon? Because the Moon *turns.* It turns just fast enough to keep the same side always toward the Earth.

For a long time people have wondered what was on the other side of the Moon. At last we know. We sent a spacecraft around the Moon. It took pictures of the other side.

Is the other side different from the side we always see?

On the Moon

On July 20, 1969, two men landed on the Moon. Astronaut Armstrong took this picture as astronaut Aldrin came out of their landing craft. ■

They had a small television camera with them. People all around the world watched.

The Moon day is hot. Aldrin and Armstrong kept cool in their space suits. They carried oxygen to breathe. They spoke to each other and to astronaut Collins by radio. He was orbiting the Moon in their spacecraft.

■

Since then other astronauts have walked on the Moon. Some explored it with a car.

This was not done just for adventure. It was done to find out things—to investigate. The astronauts set up instruments. They observed. They brought samples of rocks and sand back to Earth, as well as their observations.

Many scientists have studied the samples and observations. The scientists find no signs of water, or air, or life on the Moon. But in time they hope to find some answers. How did the Earth begin? How did the solar system begin?

LOOK BACK

1. Our nearest neighbor in space is
   planet Venus — the Moon
2. The Moon gets its light from
   the Sun — the Earth
3. Galileo looked at the Moon through a
   telescope — microscope
4. The Moon always shows us
   the same side — all its sides
5. As the Moon goes around the Earth it
   does not turn — turns slowly
6. The first men on the Moon were Aldrin and
   Collins — Armstrong

USING WHAT YOU KNOW

Make a Space Scrapbook. Use your scrapbook for cut-out pictures of spacecraft, space travel, and astronauts.

ON YOUR OWN

Look for library books about the Moon, about astronauts, about exploring space. One book you may like is *Let's Go on a Space Shuttle,* by Michael Chester, published by Putnam's, 1976. You will learn what it is like to be a member of a space shuttle crew.

Nine planets travel around the Sun. Planet Earth is one of them.

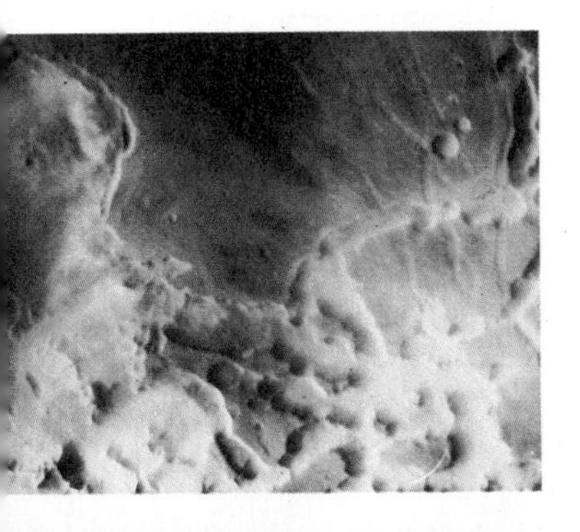

Moons travel around some of the planets. Planet Earth has one moon.

We call these planets and their moons and the Sun the solar system.

Energy from the Sun travels through space to the planets and moons. Those nearer to the Sun get more energy. Those farther from the Sun get less.

For us, planet Earth is the right distance from the Sun. We get the right amount of light and heat from the Sun's energy, for the living things we know.

We are taking our first steps away from home, out into the solar system.

Planets and moons of the solar system get energy from the Sun.

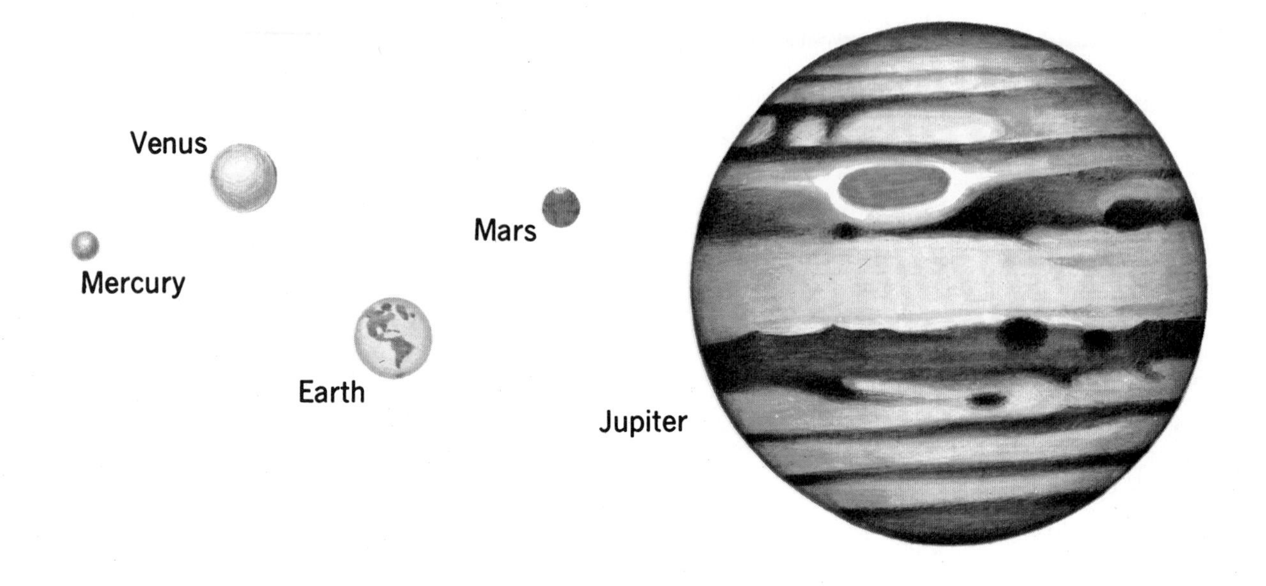

1. Which of these planets get energy from the Sun? Explain your answer.

2. Which of these planets has many green plants? How do you know?

3. Which planets get more energy from the Sun than the Earth gets? Why?

4. Which planet has many different kinds of animals? How do you know?

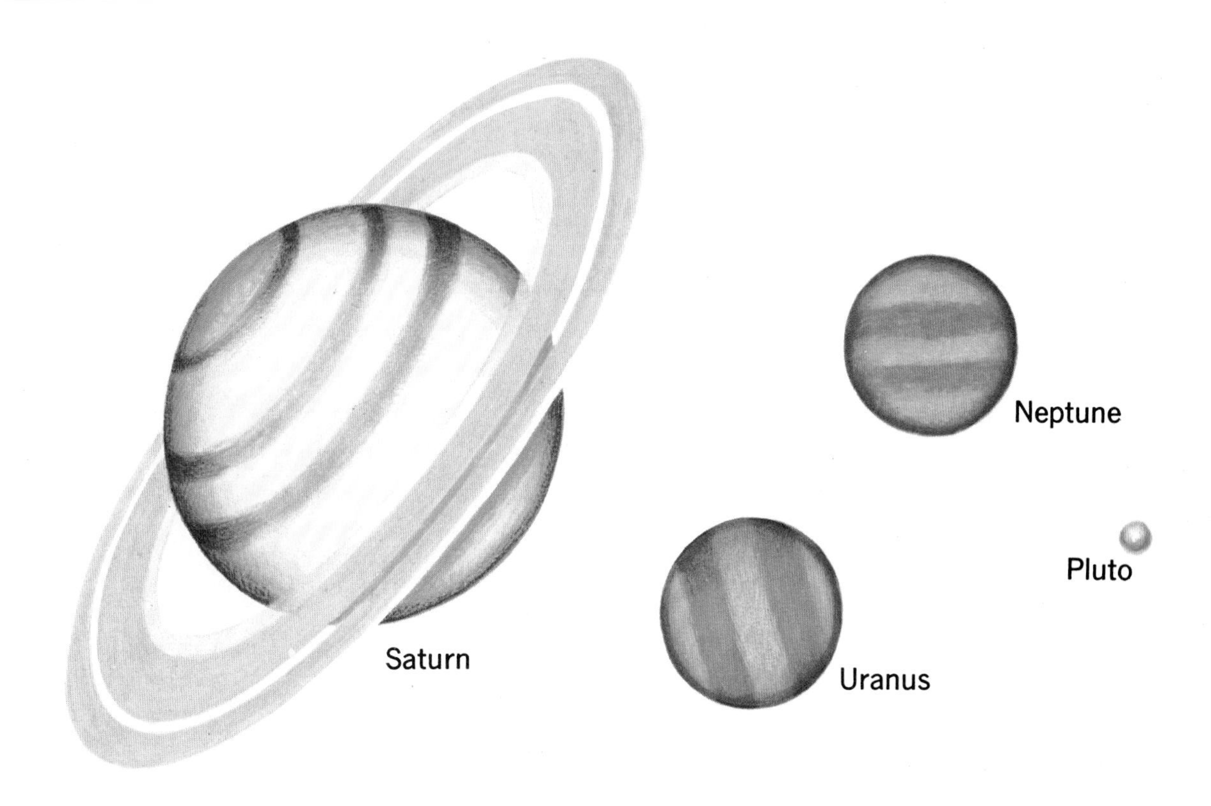

5. Which is the coldest planet? What makes you think so?

6. Which planet takes longest to go around the Sun? Why?

7. What important part of the solar system is not shown? Why is it important?

8. Which planet is the right distance from the Sun? Why do you say so?

6 / Earth's Changing Forms

What is this skater made of? Ice, of course. A block of ice was set up. Then the skater was carved out of it.

You know how ice is made. Just make water cold enough and it turns to ice. So would it be right to say that this skater is made out of water?

What is ice? Is it water? Or is it something different?

1. Changing Water

Look at this piece of water. ■

It is hard. It has a shape of its own. It is a solid, we say.

But this solid is changing, isn't it? It is melting. It is becoming a liquid. This water is changing from a solid form to a liquid form.

This water is changing its form. Do you think any water is lost when this happens? You can find out. INVESTIGATE

LEARNING TO INVESTIGATE

Is Water Lost?

Needed: A large plastic jar, ice cubes to fill it, and a scale

Fill the jar with ice cubes. ■

Put the jar on the scale. Observe where the pointer stops.

Take the jar off the scale. Cover it so that water can't escape. Put it in a warm place. Let it stand there long enough to melt all the ice. ●

Take off the cover. Don't spill any of the water! Put the jar on the scale. Observe where the pointer stops this time.

Was any water lost when it changed from solid form to liquid form?

What evidence do you have?

Can you change the liquid water to solid water? Will any water be lost?

What happens when the ice melts? The water changes from solid to liquid. But no water is lost. No water is gained.

Freeze that water. The water has changed from liquid to solid. No water is lost. No water is gained, either.

Water can change from one form to another. When it does, no water is lost and no water is gained.

Many investigations have shown this is so.

Liquid to Gas

Pour a little water into a saucer. Leave it in sunlight. You know what happens. The water slowly disappears. It evaporates.

But did you know that the disappearing water is changing its form? The water is changing from a liquid to a gas.

This gas is called water vapor. You cannot see water vapor. It has no color. But when liquid water changes to water vapor, no water is lost. However water changes form, no water is lost or gained.

LOOK BACK

1. Ice is a
   solid — liquid
2. Water turning to ice
   becomes a liquid — changes form
3. When liquid water becomes a gas, its form
   changes — does not change
4. Water vapor is the name of
   a liquid — a gas
5. When water changes form, no water
   is lost — is seen

ON YOUR OWN

Hold a piece of ice in your hand. ■

What happens to the ice? How does your hand feel? What does the ice take from your hand?

What do you think makes the ice change its form? What is your evidence?

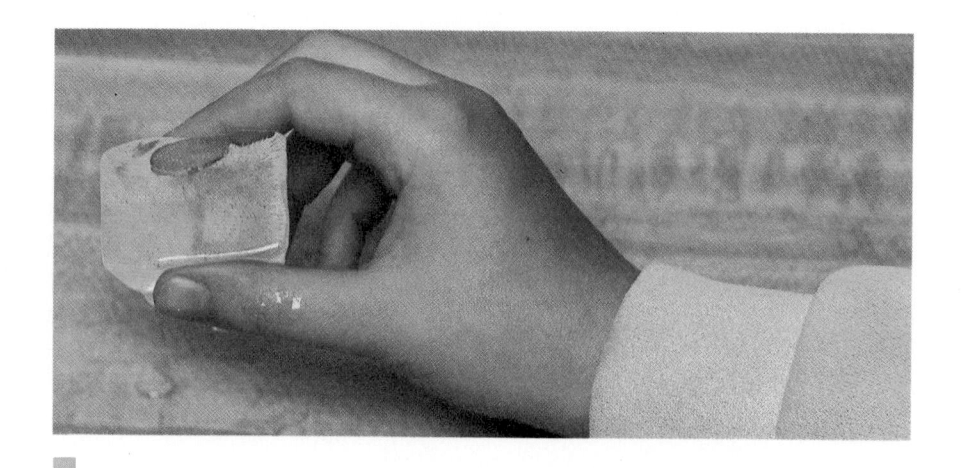

■

2. The Smallest Bits

Here are two bottles. Perfume is in one. Vinegar is in the other.

Can you tell which is which without touching them? Of course. You sniff the air over each bottle. You can tell perfume from vinegar. You use your nose.

Something from each bottle must get to your nose. Yet you can't *see* anything. What goes on here? **INVESTIGATE**

LEARNING TO INVESTIGATE

What Happens to the Perfume?

Needed: A small bottle of colored perfume, and a glass

Make sure that the glass is clean and dry.

Smell the air in the glass. Can you smell anything in the air?

Open the bottle of perfume. Put one drop of perfume on the bottom of the glass. ■

Now smell the air in the glass. Can you smell the perfume?

Observe what happens to the drop of perfume. Here is what one class observed in about an hour. ●

And an hour later. ▲

How do you explain what happened?

The drop of perfume in the glass gets smaller and smaller. It disappears. You know how: it evaporates. Tiny bits of the perfume leave the drop. They leap into the air. ■

These tiny bits are molecules. They are molecules of perfume. The molecules spread out in the air inside the glass. They keep on spreading out, into the air in the room. Some of the molecules reach your nose. You smell perfume!

Your nose is a molecule detector.

■

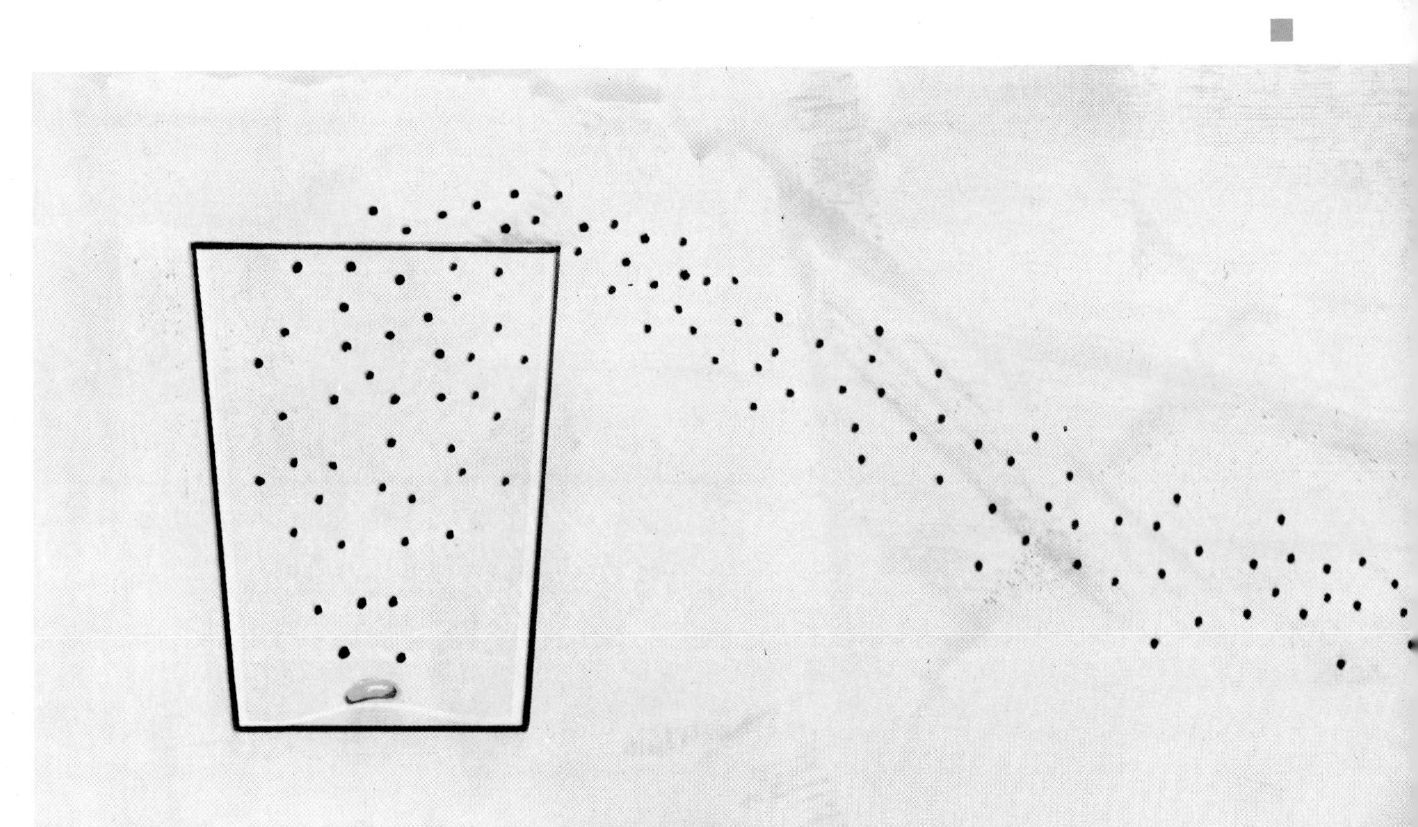

The Smallest Bit of a Thing

Perfume is a substance. So is gold. Sugar, water vapor, bananas, water—every thing is a substance. Scientists believe that substances are made up of molecules.

Scientists say that a molecule is the smallest bit of a substance there can be. The smallest bit of perfume is a molecule of perfume.

One molecule of perfume would smell like perfume. But suppose you could cut that molecule in half. Would each half smell like perfume? No. The molecule is the smallest bit of a substance.

Search on Your Own

Can you smell an onion before it is cut in half? What about after it is cut in half? Is there a difference?

How can molecules be used to explain your observations?

Make up an observation of your own. Add to your evidence about molecules.

LOOK BACK

1. Because they are so small, we cannot see
   solids molecules

2. Water and sugar are
   liquids substances

3. The smell of perfume is evidence for
   substances molecules

4. Substances are made up of
   water vapor molecules

5. The smallest bit of a substance is
   a gas a molecule

3. Mix and Separate

You know what happens when you stir sugar in water. The sugar disappears. Where does it go?

The sugar comes apart. It comes apart into the smallest bits—molecules.

The molecules of sugar are too small to be seen. But you can tell that the molecules are still there. How can you tell? You can taste the sugar in the water!

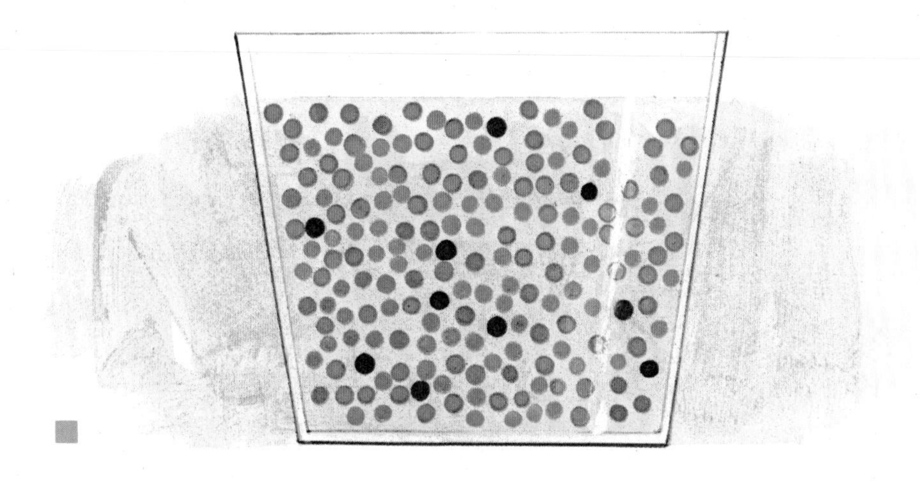

Scientists say the sugar dissolves in the water. As the sugar dissolves, the molecules of sugar scatter among the molecules of water. ■

Are those sugar molecules scattered forever? No. You can get them back. INVESTIGATE

LEARNING TO INVESTIGATE

Getting Back Molecules of Sugar

Needed: A measuring cup, a tablespoon, a pie pan, warm water, sugar

Pour water into the cup until the cup is about 1/4 full. Use warm water if you can.

Put one tablespoon of sugar into the water in the cup. Stir until all the sugar has dissolved. Put in another tablespoon of sugar. Stir until it has dissolved.

Pour the water and dissolved sugar into the pan. ■

Leave the pan in a warm place. Observe the pan each day. Here is what a class in Ohio saw on the third day. ●

How do you explain what happens?

How do you think the amount of sugar you put in will compare with the amount you get back?

How do you get back the dissolved sugar? You let the water evaporate. That separates the sugar and the water.

The sugar has not changed. Neither has the water. So the sugar and water were a mixture. In a mixture, the substances do not change.

It's easy to separate sugar and water, isn't it? Separating a mixture isn't always easy, though. Suppose you mix sugar and tiny bits of iron.

Can the mixture be separated? **INVESTIGATE**

LEARNING TO INVESTIGATE

Getting Back Iron

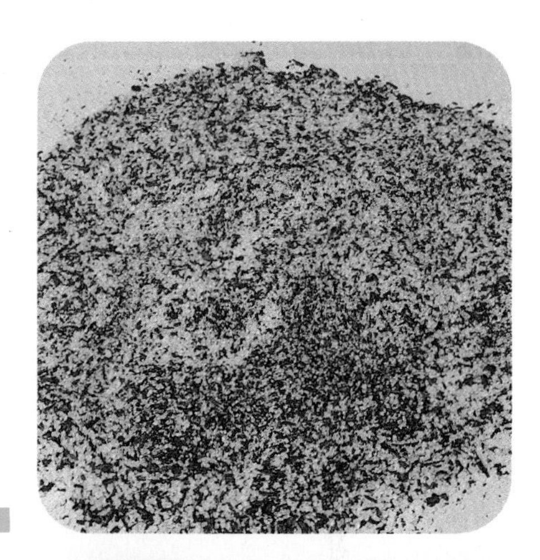

Needed: Sugar, iron filings, magnifying glass, magnet, teaspoon, piece of plain paper, piece of tissue paper

Put one teaspoon of sugar and one teaspoon of iron filings on the plain paper. Mix them. Then observe the mixture through the magnifying glass. ■

Has the sugar changed? Have the bits of iron changed?

Fold the tissue paper over the magnet. Move the magnet through the mixture. ●

What happens? ▲

Has the sugar changed? Have the bits of iron changed?

How does the magnet separate this mixture?

(Tissue paper makes it easier to get iron filings off the magnet.)

LEARNING TO INVESTIGATE

Separating Mixtures with a Filter

Needed: A jar, a rubber band, a paper towel, a teaspoon, a measuring cup, clean sand, sugar, and water

Make a filter. Push the paper towel into the jar to make a kind of bag. This is the filter. Hold it with the rubber band. ■

Fill the cup half full of water. Put in two teaspoons of sand. Stir well. Pour the mixture slowly into the filter. ●

Which goes through the filter, the sand or the water?

Clean the cup and the jar. Put in clean paper. This time dissolve two teaspoons of sugar in half a cup of water. Pour slowly into the filter.

Does the filter separate dissolved sugar and water? How can you find out?

Sand does not dissolve in water. The filter separates the solid sand from the liquid water.

But dissolved sugar goes through the filter. Remember, when sugar dissolves, it comes apart into its molecules. The molecules of sugar are so small they go through the filter.

LOOK BACK

1. When sugar dissolves, it comes apart into
   water vapor   molecules

2. The substances in a mixture
   cannot be separated   do not change

3. A magnet can separate a mixture of
   sugar and iron   sugar and water

4. A filter can separate a mixture of
   sugar and water   sand and water

5. Sugar passes through the filter when the sugar is
   solid   dissolved

USING WHAT YOU KNOW

Could you separate a mixture of iron filings, white sand, and water? Try out your plan!

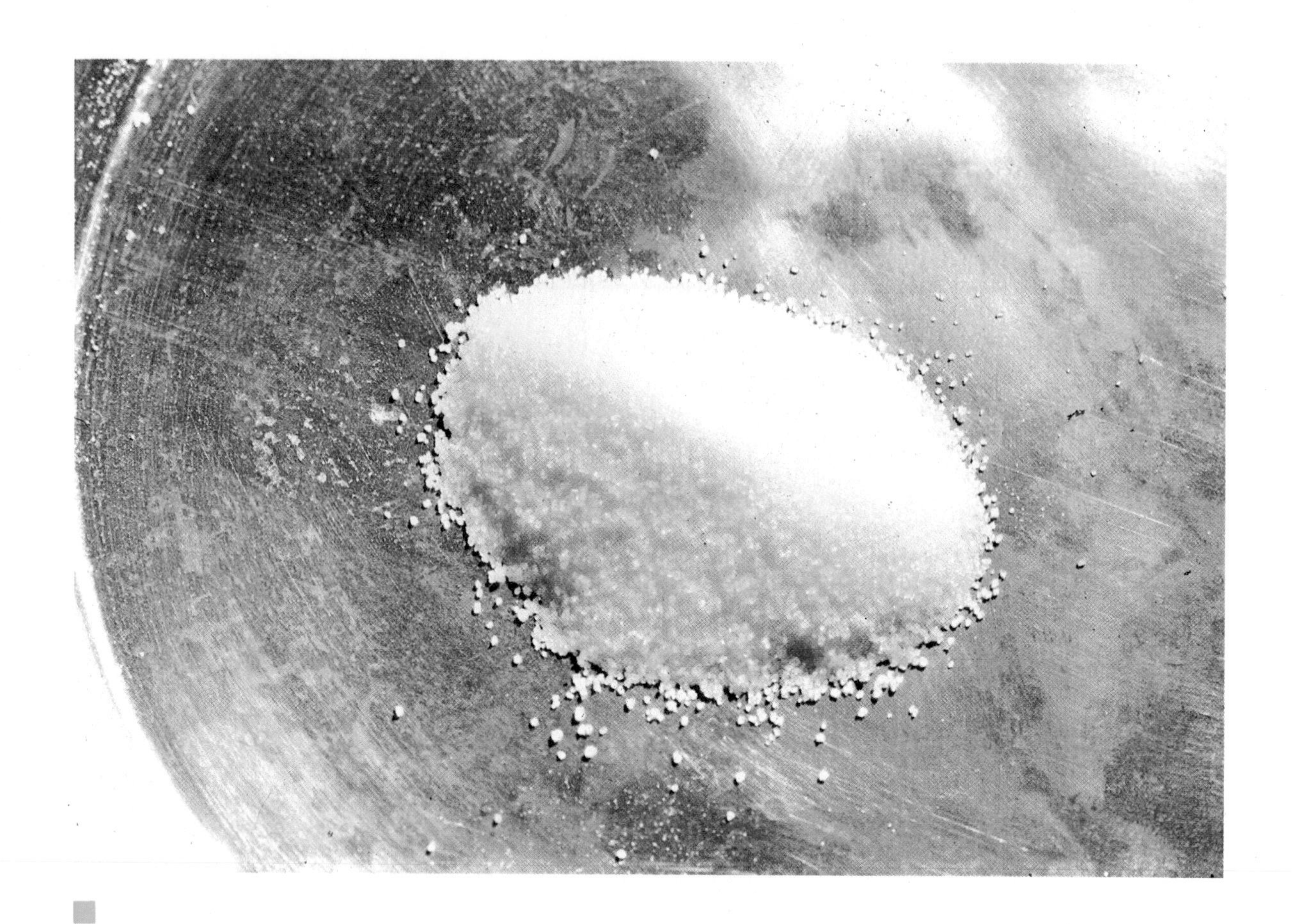

■

4. Break Up Some Molecules

Suppose you make sugar part of a mixture. The sugar molecules won't change. Or you dissolve sugar in water. The sugar molecules won't change.

But sugar molecules *can* be changed.

You can break up some sugar molecules. You can take them apart. They won't look like sugar, then. ■

What will they look like? INVESTIGATE

LEARNING TO INVESTIGATE

Breaking Up Sugar Molecules

Needed: Sugar, teaspoon, metal pie pan, electric hot plate, teacher in charge

Put the pan on the hot plate. Put one teaspoon of sugar in the pan.

Ask your teacher to turn the hot plate to *low.* Observe the sugar. It melts. Then it boils. Bubbles pop. ■

Wait until the bubbling stops. Then ask your teacher to turn off the hot plate and take the pan off. Let the pan cool. ●

Scrape the black stuff onto a sheet of white paper. ▲

Does it look like sugar? Does it taste like sugar? Taste a tiny bit. Can you dissolve it in water?

Is the black substance sugar? What evidence do you have?

■

When Sugar Molecules Break Up

That black substance is not sugar. What is it? This model of a sugar molecule will show us. ■

The molecule is made up of atoms. Each color stands for one kind of atom. How many kinds of atoms do you see?

The sugar molecule is made up of three kinds of atoms, isn't it?

When the sugar molecule gets hot enough, it comes apart. And two kinds of atoms escape. One kind is left behind.

The kind of atom left behind is carbon. That black substance left in the pan is carbon.

Our model of a sugar molecule can show us something else. Remember that you see bubbles as the sugar is heated. Those bubbles are giving off water vapor. Here's where the water comes from.

The sugar molecule is heated. It comes apart. Carbon atoms are left in the pan. But there are two other kinds of atoms in the sugar molecule. They are hydrogen atoms and oxygen atoms.

These hydrogen atoms and oxygen atoms come together. They form molecules of water. ●

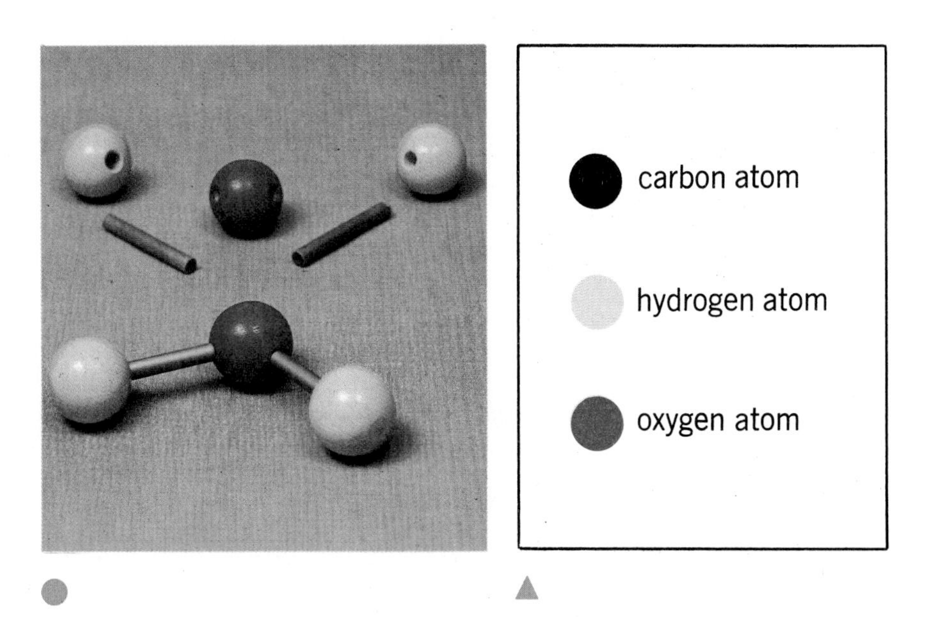

● ▲

Now you can tell what atoms make up that model of a molecule of sugar. ▲

LOOK BACK

1. We can get carbon by heating
   water   sugar

2. Heating sugar can break up its
   molecules   atoms

3. A sugar molecule is made of
   smaller molecules   atoms

4. A sugar molecule that breaks up
   is not sugar   is still sugar

5. We can get water by heating
   sugar   carbon

ON YOUR OWN

Break up more molecules. Put 1/4 cup of vinegar into a bottle. Add 1 teaspoon of baking soda bit by bit. A new substance will appear, a gas! It will bubble up. Vinegar and baking soda both change when they are put together.

●

▲

5. Different Kinds of Changes

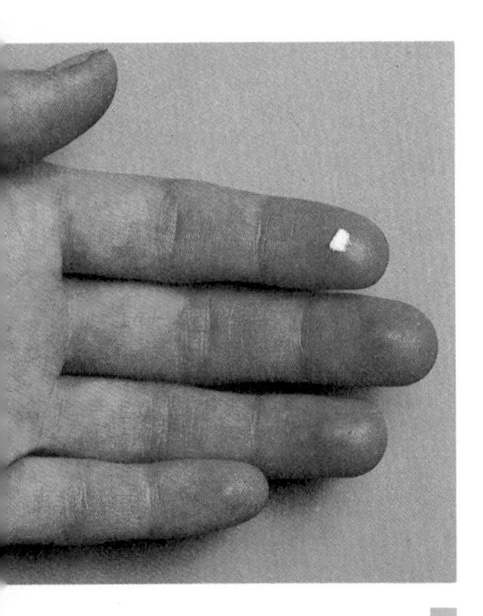

■

Tear a sheet of paper in half. Tear one of the pieces in half. Keep on tearing until you have a very tiny piece. ■

You change the size of the paper. You change its shape. But it is still paper. Its molecules have not changed.

What about this paper? ●

What's left when the flame goes out? ▲

Is it still paper? No. The molecules have changed. Burning made the molecules break up.

Kinds of Changes

There are two kinds of changes, aren't there?

You break a piece of wood. You dissolve some sugar. You are changing sizes and shapes. But you still have wood and sugar. The molecules have not changed. This kind of change is a physical change. ■

You burn a piece of wood. It changes to other substances. Its molecules have changed. You heat sugar. It changes to other substances. Its molecules have changed. This kind of change is a chemical change. ●

LOOK BACK

Is it a physical change or a chemical change?

1. A candle is cut into pieces.
2. A candle is burning.
3. A candle left in sunlight is melting.
4. An ice cube is melting.
5. Sugar is dissolving in water.
6. Gasoline is burning in a motor.
7. A piece of rock is being broken up.
8. Water in a pot is boiling away.

ON YOUR OWN

Wrap two iron nails in a wet paper towel. Put them into an open jar. Keep the paper damp. After a few days look for a reddish brown substance on the nails and on the paper. It means that molecules are changing. Atoms of iron and atoms of oxygen are coming together to make a new substance. Do you know what it is?

6. Earth's Most Important Substances?

What are Earth's two most important substances? Gold and silver? Money and diamonds?

What about air? Could we live without it? No, not for more than a few moments. We depend on air. So do animals. So do plants. What about water? We depend on water, too.

Air and water are different, aren't they? As different as they are, they are alike in one way. We are having trouble with Earth's stores of air and water.

What's happening here to our store of air? ■

The air is changing. Some days, around big cities, it stings people's eyes. Some days it is hard for people to breathe. Trees and other plants cannot grow well in it.

What's happening? Chimneys pour smoke into the air, as you see. They pour invisible gases into the air, too. And our automobile engines pour great amounts of invisible gases into the air.

So the air is becoming dirty, or polluted. Earth's store of air is becoming more polluted each year.

Earth's store of water is becoming polluted too. How? **INVESTIGATE**

LEARNING TO INVESTIGATE

What Happens to Polluted Water?

Needed: Pie pan, teaspoon, water, different kinds of waste materials

Fill the pan half full of water.

Put in a teaspoon of coffee grounds. Add a bit of banana skin. Add some oil.

Add a few drops of nail polish and a few rubber bands. (Think of them as old tires.) Add a bit of dishwashing detergent. Add some bits of egg shell.

Add a little milk and some margarine. Put in small bits of plastic. ■

Observe what happens as the water evaporates. Do other substances evaporate too? ●

Add clean water. Does the water in the pan stay polluted? How do you explain this?

Polluted Water

In the investigation, water becomes polluted. Much the same thing is happening to the Earth's water. We are putting in too much waste material. Earth's water is becoming more and more polluted.

Some waste material does not pollute water. Some is used as food by animals that live in water. Some settles to the bottom and is buried. But some waste material makes water unfit for living things.

Oil, garbage, and other wastes are flowing into our rivers. Many rivers are now ugly. Some are dangerous.

Lakes that were for swimming are now fenced off. Their water is polluted. Even the wide oceans are getting polluted. Beaches that were for swimming are fenced off.

We pour our waste material into our air and water. Once it didn't seem to matter. Now we know it does matter.

Can we keep substances that are bad for living things out of our water and air? Scientists are trying to find ways of doing this. We need new ways of getting rid of our waste material. We must stop polluting Earth's two most important substances, air and water.

Search on Your Own

How much waste material do you and your family make in a week?

Plan an investigation. You don't need a very accurate answer. Weigh one bundle. Then guess the weight of other bundles. Should you count the water you use as waste?

You may be in for a shock.

LOOK BACK

1. Air and water are needed by

   all things — living things

2. Air and water unfit for living things are

   clean — polluted

3. Water is polluted by

   waste material — evaporation

4. Air is often polluted around

   big cities — big forests

5. Most engines that burn gasoline

   clean the air — pollute the air

ON YOUR OWN

Gasoline engines take in air. They take in air through filters. What do the filters catch? Ask some questions and see what you can find out.

one more time

The Earth is a storehouse of substances. The substances are made of molecules. The molecules are made of atoms.

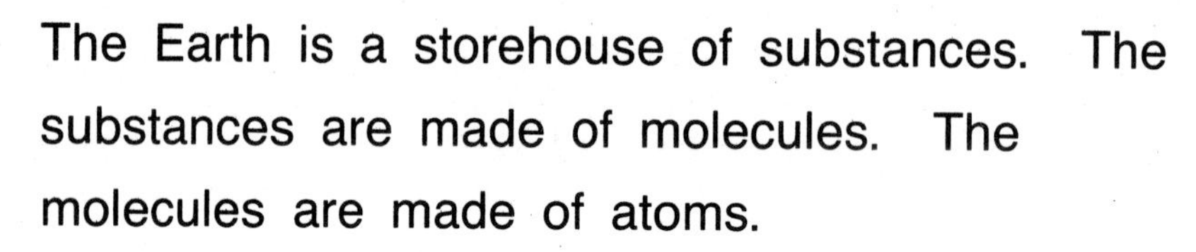

Some of Earth's substances are in gas form. Some are in liquid form. Some are in solid form. Substances can change from one form to another.

A substance may change in form or size or shape, and still be the same substance. Its molecules have not changed. This is a physical change.

A substance may change as its molecules break up. The atoms form new molecules. New substances are formed. This is a chemical change.

Substances are made up of atoms and molecules.
Substances can be changed.

Answer these questions about each picture.

1. What is changing?
2. Is it a physical change or a chemical change?
3. From your own observations, what evidence do you have for your answers?

7/Fitness To Live

You can tell that these wings are shaped for flying, can't you?

An albatross spends most of its time in the air. It is an expert at soaring above the waters, looking for food.

Its eyes are sharp. Its beak is good for catching fish. Its feet fold up out of the way in flight. But they are good paddles when it moves in water.

Is the albatross fitted to fly? Is it fitted to find food? What does this mean, to be fitted?

Begin your probe. Turn the page.

1. Fitness

There are scientists who study how living things are fitted for life. They find things like this. They find that different birds have different kinds of feet. ■

Which feet are for holding on to a branch? Which are for swimming and wading? Why do you say so?

■

■

Now study these birds. Which one has feet fitted for holding? Which bird is fitted for swimming or wading?

By the way, look at those beaks. Which beak is fitted for tearing flesh? Which is fitted for scooping up things from water? Why do you say so?

Here are two different beaks.

Which beak is best fitted to crack the tough cover of a seed?

Which beak is fitted for sucking up liquid from deep inside a flower? Why do you say so?

●

▲

Yes, that long, thin beak is best fitted for dipping into flowers. Have you ever seen the ruby-throated hummingbird feeding? ●

That tough, blunt beak is fitted for cracking seeds. Have you seen English sparrows at work? ▲

Here's a strange beak! What do you think it is best fitted for? When you are sure of your reasoning, turn the page and see if you are right. ◆

◆

Fitness in an Insect

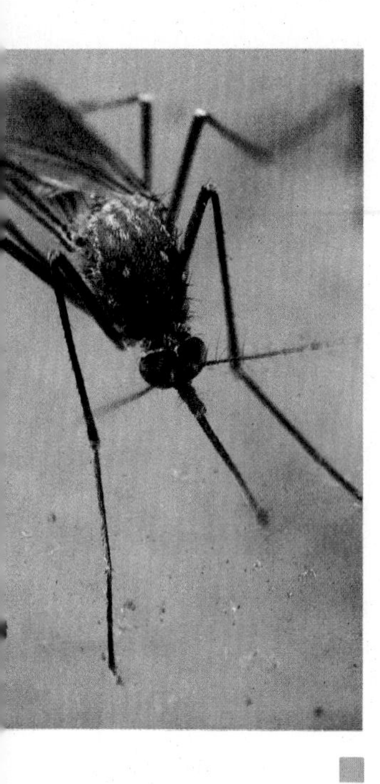

Here is one insect's way of getting food. ■

Here is another insect's way of getting its food. ●

Which insect is fitted to chew on plants? Which is fitted to stab through your skin? What is your reasoning?

That needle is the mouth of a mosquito. The tough, biting mouth parts belong to a grasshopper.

Do you think you have an idea of what fitness means? Find out. **INVESTIGATE**

■

●

Answer: The beak is used to poke in the sand for food. The bird is an avocet.

LEARNING TO INVESTIGATE

Fitness—On Land, in Water

Needed: a small fish in a tank, a pet such as a rabbit (a guinea pig, dog, or cat will do just as well)

How is this living thing fitted for life in water? ■

How is this living thing fitted for life on land? ●

Study your living things. Probe these questions.

—How is one fitted to get air from water? How is the other fitted to get air on land?

—How are they fitted to move, in water and on land?

—How are they fitted to get food, in water and on land?

Make up a question of your own about fitness of these living things. Then answer your own question.

Search on Your Own

There is one living thing you know well: you. Do you really know how you are fitted to live?

Find out how you are fitted to live in many environments—warm and cold, water and land. Find out how your hand or your voice, for example, fits you to do things no other living thing can do.

LOOK BACK

Match the words and the pictures of parts of living things. You may want to use the same words more than once. Give your reasoning.

Fitted for water

Fitted for land

Fitted for grabbing

Fitted for jumping

Fitted for tearing

2. Fitness to Live—In a Pond

Plants grow in ponds, as you know. Some plants are tiny, like these algae. ■ Algae are food for most animals that live in a pond. Young fish depend on algae for their food.

All the plants in the picture are alike in one way, however. They are green plants. Like all green plants, these green plants make food.

The animals that live in a pond depend on the food the green plants make.

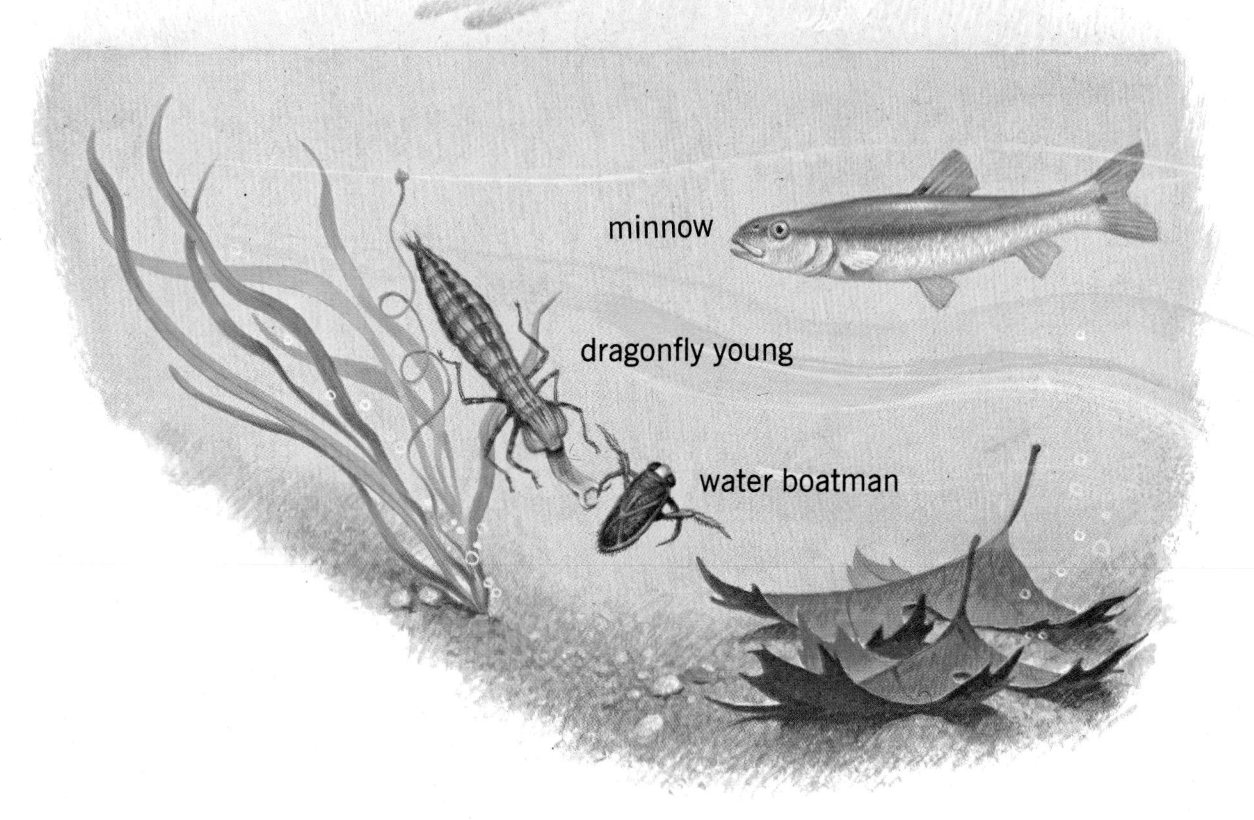

Fitness to Live—in Water

The dragonfly is hunting for food.

It catches mosquitoes and flies and other insects in the air. But it lays eggs only in water. Dragonfly young hatch from the eggs.

Dragonfly young breathe through gills. The gills take air out of the water. How are the dragonfly young fitted to live in water?

One day a dragonfly young crawls out of the water. It works itself out of its skin. It begins to breathe air. It spreads shiny wings. It is an adult dragonfly. How is it fitted to live now?

The diving beetle lays eggs. The young are called water tigers. A water tiger has strong jaws. It can catch an animal bigger than itself.

The water tiger has gills in its tail. Do you think the water tiger has to come up for air? What is your reasoning?

How are water tigers and dragonfly young fitted for life under water?

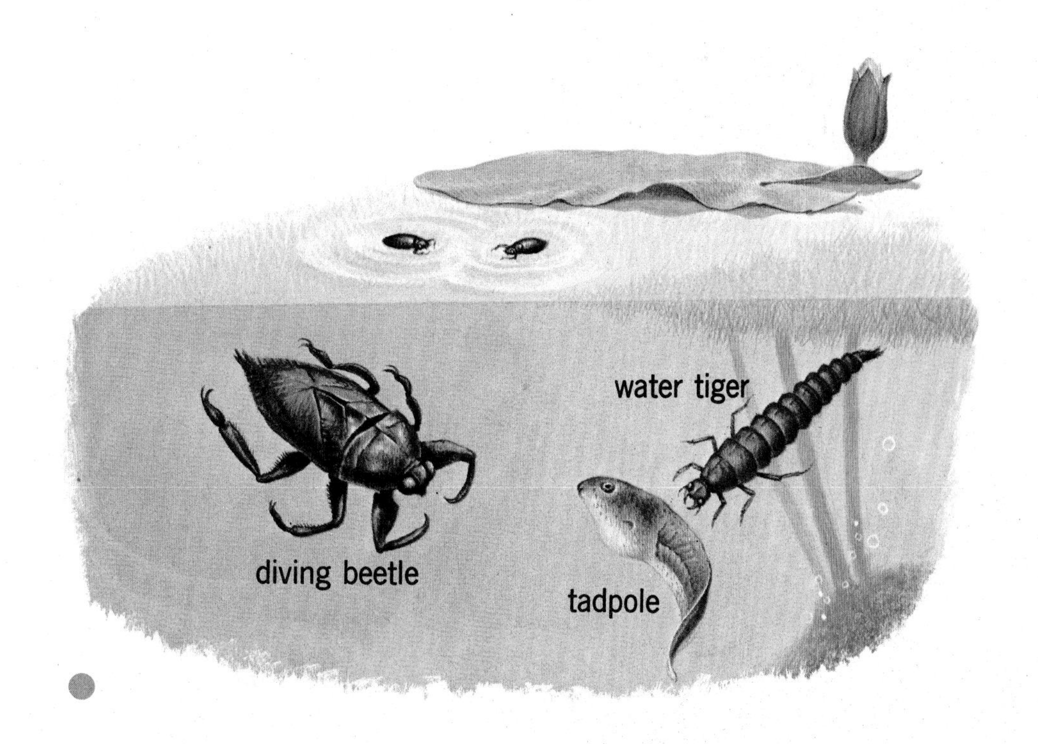

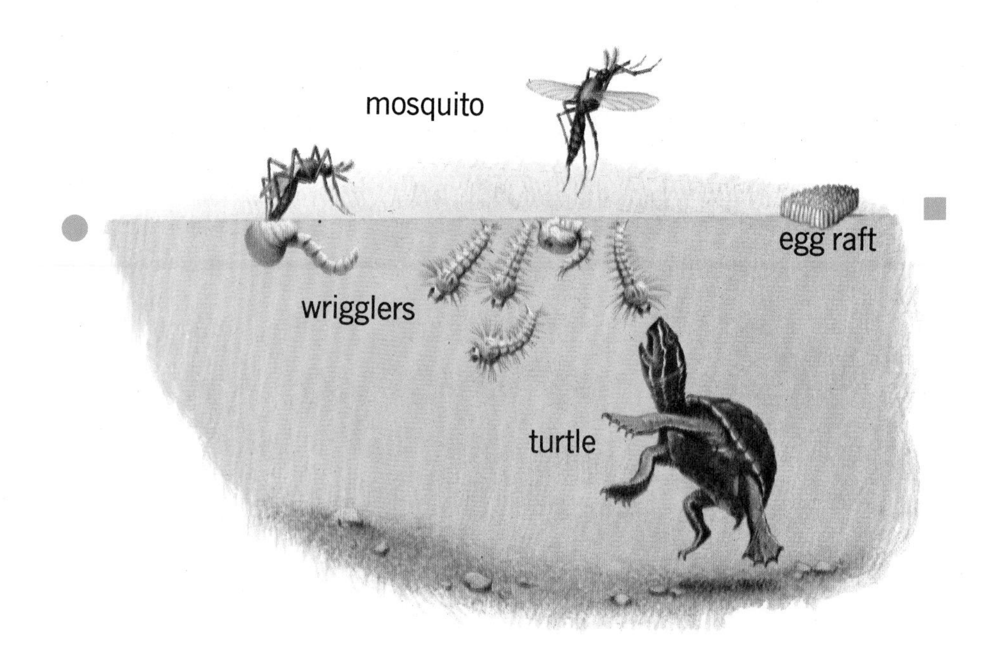

Still Another Way

Mosquitoes lay flat rafts of eggs. ■

The young wriggle up and down in the water. Sometimes they are called wrigglers.

Wrigglers do not have gills. A wriggler wriggles tail first to the top of the water. It puts a breathing tube into the air. Then it wriggles back down. If it cannot reach the air, it will die. ●

Suppose you wanted to get rid of mosquitoes. What might you do? Here is a clue: How is the wriggler fitted to get air? What might you do to keep wrigglers from getting air? (When you think of an answer, see On Your Own on page 216.)

Other Signs of Fitness

You may see some mollusks in the pond. They are animals with soft bodies and hard shells. There may be pond snails. When the snail is frightened it can pull back into its shell. How is the snail fitted to protect itself? ▲

You may see fish. Shiny minnows dart here and there. Bigger fish hunt smaller ones. How are they fitted to protect themselves? ♦

In any pond there are different living things. And each of them is somehow fitted to live in its environment.

What is your environment? How are you fitted to live in it?

LOOK BACK

1. The green plants in a pond
   can make food — cannot make food

2. Dragonfly young are fitted to live in
   water — air

3. A water tiger can stay under water because it has
   strong jaws — gills

4. Wrigglers are fitted to live in water by their
   gills — tubes

5. The pond is an environment for
   one living thing — many living things

ON YOUR OWN

Put some water in a glass. Then put in a drop or two of oil. Salad oil or machine oil will do. What happens to the oil?

The oil puts a kind of lid on the water. A wriggler cannot get through this lid. The wriggler will die. Why will it die?

3. Fitness to Live—In the Seas

Have you seen seaweeds that have been washed onto the beach? ■

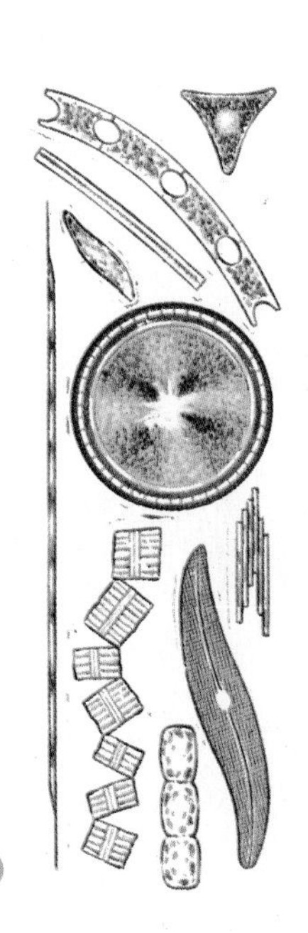

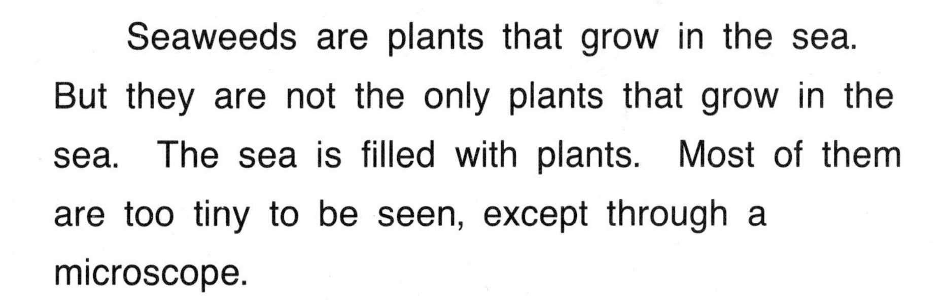

Seaweeds are plants that grow in the sea. But they are not the only plants that grow in the sea. The sea is filled with plants. Most of them are too tiny to be seen, except through a microscope.

Here are some of the tiny plants, many times their real size. How are they like algae? ●

They are green plants. They have chlorophyll. The chlorophyll uses energy from sunlight to make the plants' food.

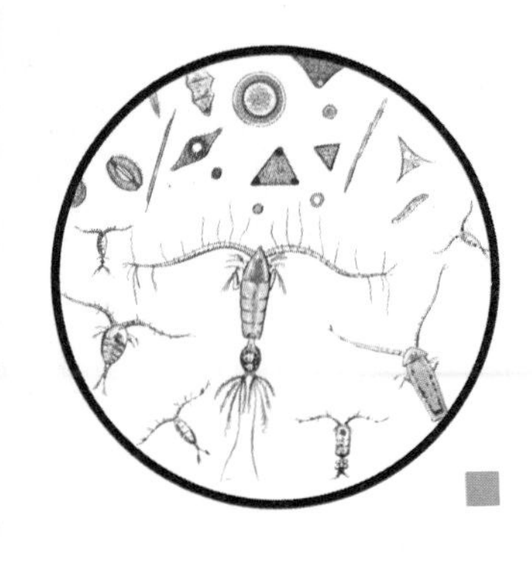

There are tiny animals in the sea, as well as tiny plants.

What do you suppose these tiny animals feed on? Tiny plants. Then the tiny animals are used as food by larger animals. The larger animals are eaten by still larger animals, and so on! In this way the food made by the tiny green plants is used by the animals in the sea.

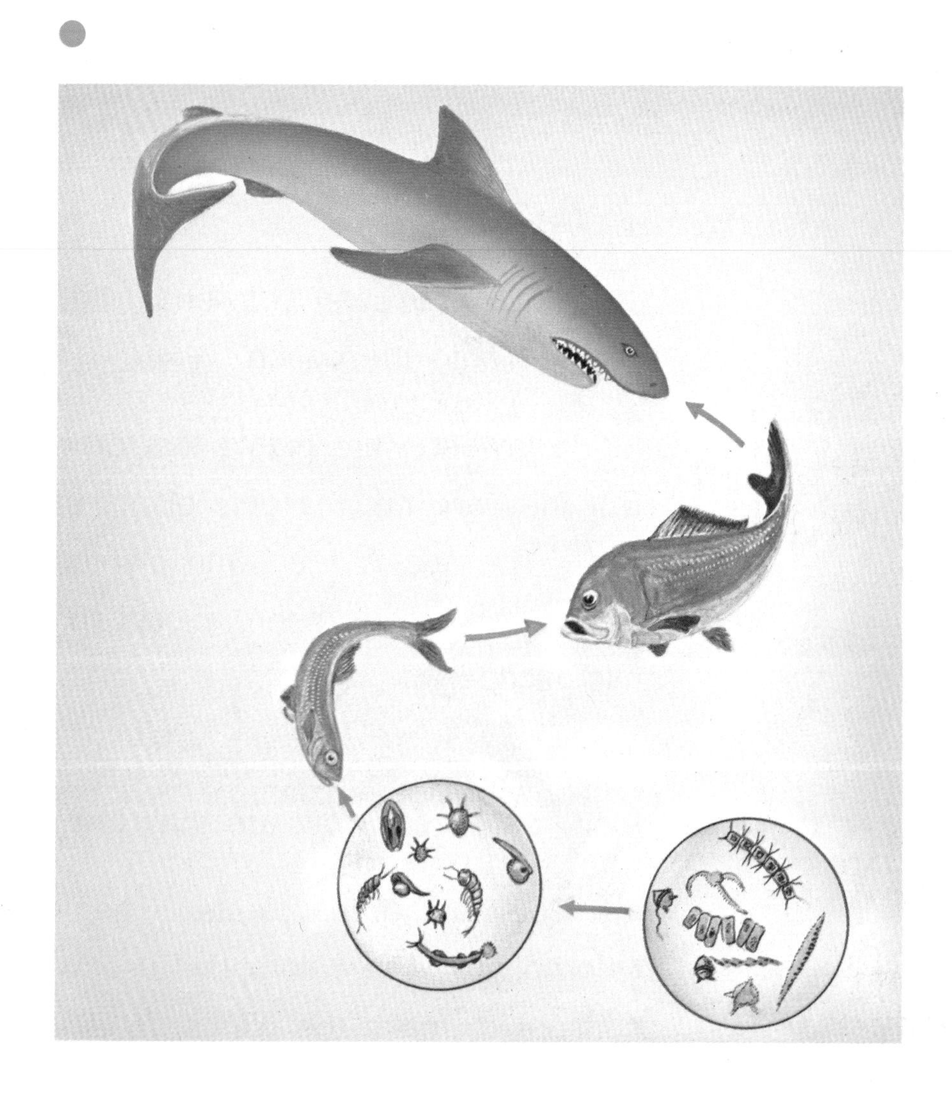

▲

Fitness—In Icy Seas

The coldest land on the Earth is Antarctica. Antarctica's ice and snow never melt. Yet animals live in Antarctica. Look at this finback whale. ▲

The finback whale is a very large mammal indeed. Yet it feeds on sea animals the size of grasshoppers. They feed on tiny plants.

Every summer the tiny plants and animals drift towards Antarctica. The finback whale follows its food. How can it live in the icy water? One reason is that its body has a thick layer of fat. The fat keeps the whale warm. What do you do to keep warm?

The whale lives only in water. Yet it is not a fish. The whale is a mammal. It comes to the top of the water to breathe air.

A baby whale is called a calf. The calf gets milk from its mother. The mother takes care of the calf until it is grown.

Another mammal that lives in Antarctica is the seal. Seals spend most of their time in water. Like the whale, the seal has a thick layer of fat. Fat and fur help keep the seal warm. ■

Baby seals are called pups. Seal pups get milk from the mother. The mother seal feeds on fish. Do you know of other pups that get milk from the mother?

■

These are the biggest penguins in the world.

Some are more than a meter tall. They are Emperor penguins, found only in Antarctica.

In the icy water, Emperor penguins catch fish for food. How can penguins stand the cold? A thick layer of fat helps keep them warm. Also, they are covered with thick, oily feathers that shed water.

Once a year the female penguin lays one egg. When the egg hatches, the parents feed fish to the chick.

In Warm Seas

What are these strange branches under water? ■

They are not plants. They are coral. They are made by tiny coral animals. A coral animal has a soft body shaped like an open bag. The opening is its mouth.

Coral animals live together. When they die, hard coral material is left behind. Different kinds of coral animals make different shapes of coral.

For many thousands of years hard coral has built up in warm seas. Walls of coral have formed under water. They are called coral reefs.

■

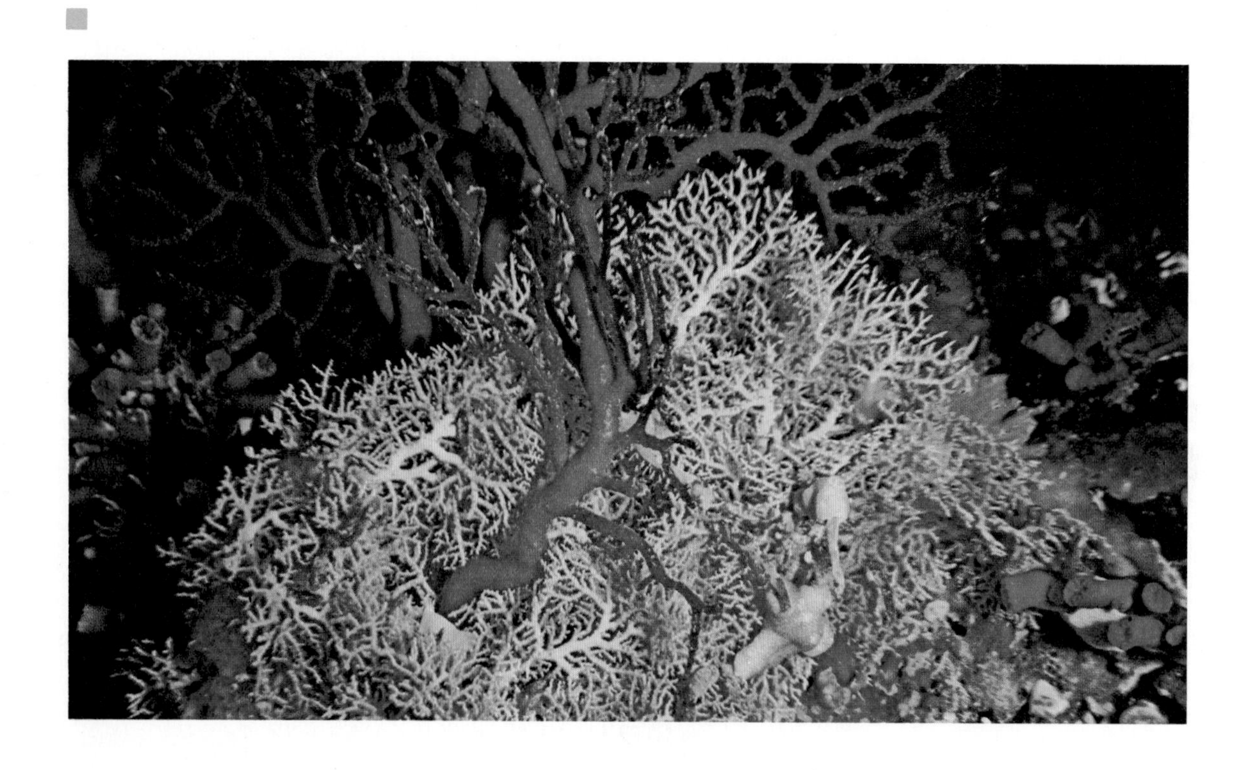

A Visit to a Coral Reef

You are in a boat that has a large window in the bottom. The boat moves over a coral reef.

Bright colored fish swim in and out. Do you see something like a flower? It is an animal, a sea anemone. Its tentacles are for catching food.

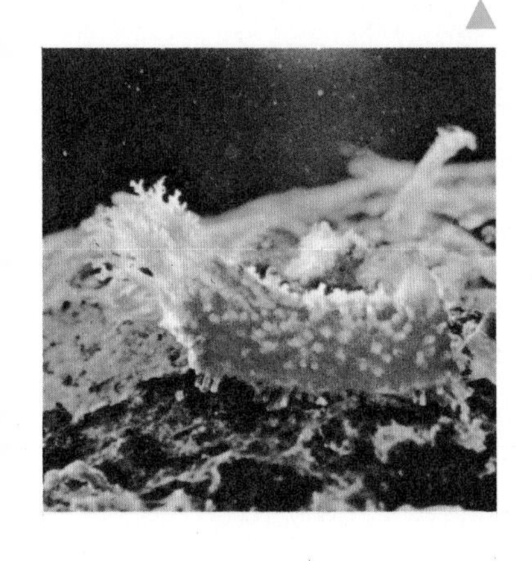

There is a sea cucumber lying on the bottom. This spiny animal has tentacles around its mouth. There are many kinds of animals with soft bodies and hard shells. And there are starfish.

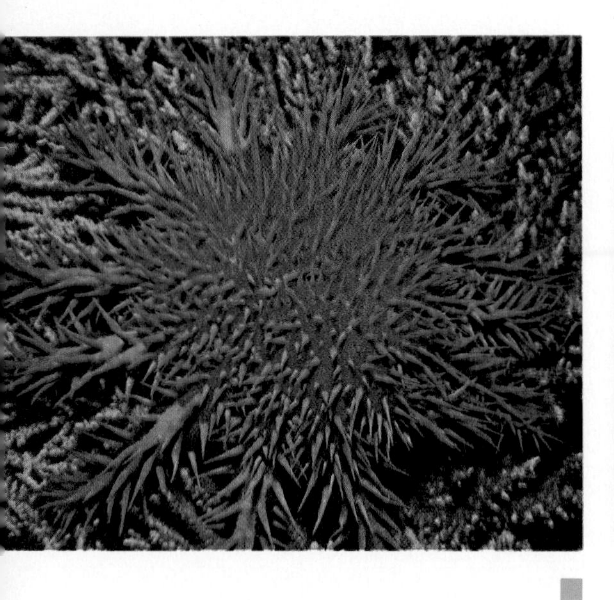

Too Many Starfish?

Why do you think this starfish is called the crown-of-thorns? ■

The crown-of-thorns feeds on coral animals. Sometimes too many starfish eat too many coral animals. This changes the coral reef environment. Many sea animals depend on that environment.

Giant tritons feed on starfish. ● But the tritons are hunted for their shells. Not enough tritons may mean too many starfish. Why?

Scientists are looking for ways to conserve the coral reefs. If they save the reefs, they will save the animals that live in the reefs.

Search on Your Own

Visit a store that sells aquarium supplies. Look at some tropical fish.

Why do their aquariums have heaters? Air pumps? Are there some other living things in their aquariums? Why? What sort of food do the tropical fish need?

Put together a picture of the environment from which a tropical fish came.

LOOK BACK

1. Seaweeds are plants that grow
   on the beach — in the sea
2. Green plants in the sea need
   darkness — sunlight
3. A baby whale is fitted for life in cold seas by its layer of
   scales — fat
4. Emperor penguins are covered with
   feathers — fur
5. Coral is made by
   a plant — an animal

4. Fitness to Live—On Land

Think of the land today, filled with plants and animals and people.

Plants were the first to grow on land. Then came animals. Today plants and animals live together in many different environments. Let's look at some different environments.

Grasslands

Grassland soil is deep and rich. Grass grows well there year after year. There may be trees here and there. There are rivers and lakes, low hills and grassy meadows.

Today cattle and sheep feed on grasslands. In many places the land is used for farming. Corn and wheat and other crops are planted. Farms, ranches, towns, and cities have spread out on the grasslands.

There have been other changes in this environment. Do you know this animal?

Its true name is bison. Once there were many bison on the grasslands. Then white hunters killed thousands of them for hides and sport. The pioneers killed bison to make way for ranches and farms. The bison were becoming extinct. There were only a few hundred left.

At last laws were made to protect bison. Once people nearly destroyed this animal. Now we are saving it. How did the grasslands environment change for the bison?

Home in the Ground

Here is another animal that lives in the grasslands environment. Can you name it? ■

These small animals are called prairie dogs. But they are not dogs. They are members of the ground squirrel family.

Prairie dogs dig their homes in the ground. Each home has a number of rooms.

■

One room is for food. Prairie dogs gather up seeds, leaves, and roots of grass plants. They store away some of this food for winter use.

A prairie dog watches for other animals that hunt it. It watches for coyotes. ● It watches for rattlesnakes, and for hawks and eagles and owls. ▲

At a sign of danger, the prairie dog makes a loud whistling sound. This warns other prairie dogs. Then it hides in its underground home.

Can prairie dogs live where there is no grass? How is their environment changing?

Forests

Let's look at a very different environment.

Rain falls often. The air is moist and still. It is hot. This kind of forest is a jungle.

In this jungle, monkeys chatter. Parrots give strange cries. An anteater walks with its nose to the ground. A snake slides toward a frog. A jungle cat is ready to spring.

The jungle is crowded with plants and animals. How do they live in this environment?

This forest is also a busy place.

There are different trees. Low plants are on the ground. There are mosses and ferns and fungi. The soil is rich and damp.

Once we had many such forests in America. They were filled with bears, foxes, rabbits, deer, and other animals. But as forests are cut down, there are fewer forest animals.

In our national parks, trees and animals are protected. You might see bears there, for example. The forest is their natural environment. How do they live in it?

Bears catch fish in forest streams. They take honey from the hives of wild bees. Their thick fur protects them from stings.

In summer bears eat berries and roots and tender leaves. In a national park they may even stop cars and beg for food! But bears are dangerous. ***Never go near a bear.***

By summer's end bears are fat. When the days get cold, they find a cave. They go to sleep there. They live on fat stored in their bodies.

In early spring the bears come out. They are thin and hungry. With them are new cubs.

Deserts

Suppose you are hiking across this desert in Arizona.

The soil is sandy and rocky. You see a cactus and other strange, prickly plants. There are many days when the air is hot and still. There are cold days too. There are days when the wind blows sharp sand across the land.

It may rain here only once a year. Dry as the desert is, it has its own plants and animals. They live together in this desert environment. How do they do it?

Desert plants can grow with little water. Cactus plants store water in thick stems. ■

Plants lose water through their leaves. But most desert plants have tiny leaves or no leaves. So they lose little water.

Desert plants may have long roots to reach underground water.

Some desert animals feed only on plants. ● A spiny cactus is a juicy meal for a tortoise. ▲ Small fruits and seeds are food for desert birds. ◆ Plant eaters are hunted by meat eaters. ★

A tortoise gets water from the plants it eats. Desert birds and animals get water from what they eat.

Animals and plants, all depend on their desert environment. Can you tell how?

jack rabbit

California quail

desert horned lizard

Cities

Food comes to cities. People in cities depend on plants and animals outside cities.

Does this mean that there are no plants and animals that live in a city? Let's look at the environment of a city.

Perhaps you live in a city. How many different kinds of trees can you see? Never mind if you do not know their names. How many different kinds of plants do you see sharing your city environment?

sparrow

pigeon

starling

grackle

How many different birds can you observe?

How do birds live in the city environment? How do they get food? Where do they nest? Where do they get water?

ants

ladybug

clothes moth

cricket

What other kinds of animals live in a city environment? Look in grass and soil. Look in flowers and weeds and shrubs. Look indoors as well.

Some city animals are pests. Pests annoy us or harm us. The cockroach is an insect pest. So is the housefly, the bedbug, the mosquito. Rats and mice are mammals that are pests.

Many insects are not pests. Look for bees, butterflies, and ladybug beetles. Spiders and earthworms are not pests.

Where do these city animals get food? Here is a clue to an answer.

Caterpillars feed mainly on leaves. Bees use nectar and pollen from flowers for food. Garden snails feed on plants.

Earthworms take in soil through their mouths. In the soil are plant and animal materials. Earthworms use these materials for food.

As long as plants grow in a city, there is food for many kinds of animals. Plants and animals live together. They all depend on the city environment. So do the people living in a city.

LOOK BACK

1. The soil is deep and rich in
   grasslands deserts
2. For food prairie dogs gather up
   cactus plants grass plants
3. One kind of forest environment is
   a grassland a jungle
4. The plants in a desert environment grow with
   little water no water

5. In a city environment animals
   can't live can live
6. An environment
   can change can't change

INVENT AN ENVIRONMENT

Suppose you could have any animal or plant you wanted for your own. It would live with you. You would take care of it.

What would you choose for your own? For what reasons? How would you make a good environment for it?

one more time

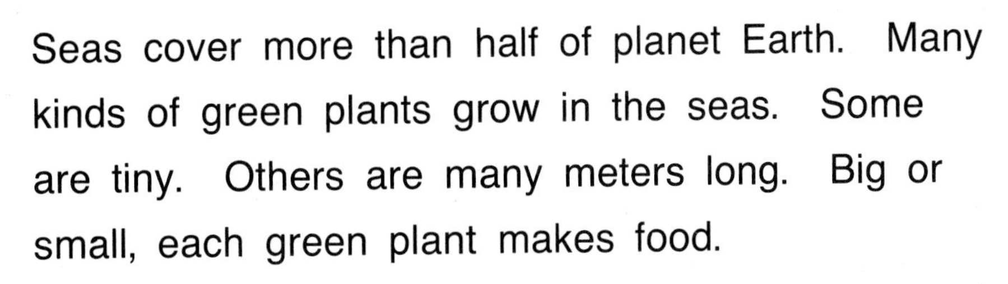

Seas cover more than half of planet Earth. Many kinds of green plants grow in the seas. Some are tiny. Others are many meters long. Big or small, each green plant makes food.

Fish and many other kinds of animals live in the seas. They feed on green sea plants and on one another.

On land, food is made by green plants. There are many different kinds of land plants. Each plant is fitted to live in its own environment.

Land animals, like sea animals, feed on green plants. And they feed on each other.

Land plants and animals are not fitted to the sea environment. Sea plants and animals are not fitted to the land environment. Each living thing must find what it needs for life in its environment.

Each kind of living thing is fitted to live in its own kind of environment.

From the list below, choose the best environment for each of the animals shown.

hot, sandy desert	grassland
icy, cold sea	city park or yard
fresh-water pond	hot, moist jungle

Explain how each animal gets something it needs from its environment.

We travel in space on planet Earth.

Planet Earth gives us what we need for life. We depend on Earth's coal, oil, and gas. We depend on its iron and copper. We depend on its nitrogen and sulfur. We depend on its soil.

Surely this planet is our home—our only home.

Earth is also the home of many different plants and animals. Surely we must conserve its plants and animals. We must conserve its air, water, and soil, its fuels and minerals. Surely we must take care of this small, beautiful planet. Do we have another choice?

We have no choice but to use Earth's stores wisely. We have no choice but to keep our environment healthy.

For where else can we get what we need for life?

The Metric System of Measurement

Scientists and most people of the world use the metric system of measurement. Before long, we in the United States will be using the metric system in our daily lives.

The metric system is also called the International System, abbreviated **SI.** In this system, scientists measure in the following standard units:

length in **meters**
weight in **newtons**
mass in **grams**
volume in **liters**
temperature in degrees **Celsius**

In the metric system, several prefixes are important:

centi = hundredth (0.01)
milli = thousandth (0.001)
kilo = thousand (1000)

Once you know these prefixes, you can use the system easily. Each unit of the metric system can be divided by 10 to find the next smaller unit. For example, one meter is divided into 10 parts, each part called a decimeter (the prefix **deci** means tenth). A decimeter can be divided into 10 parts, each called a centimeter. When centimeters are divided by 10, each part is called a millimeter. One meter, then, is equal to 10 decimeters, 100 centimeters, and 1,000 millimeters. And 1,000 meters are equal to one kilometer.

The diagrams on these two pages will help you become more familiar with the metric system.

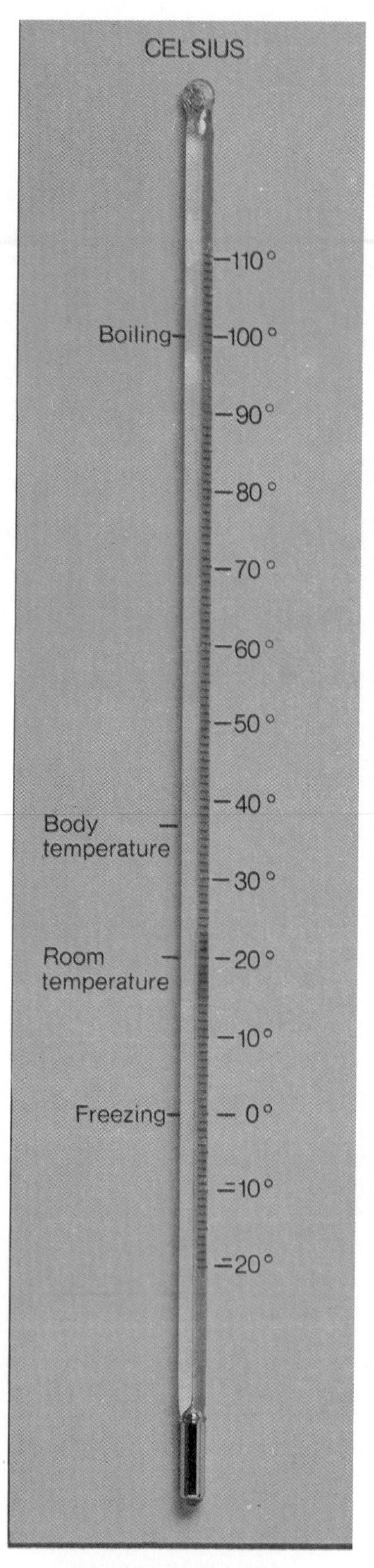

TEMPERATURE

LENGTH

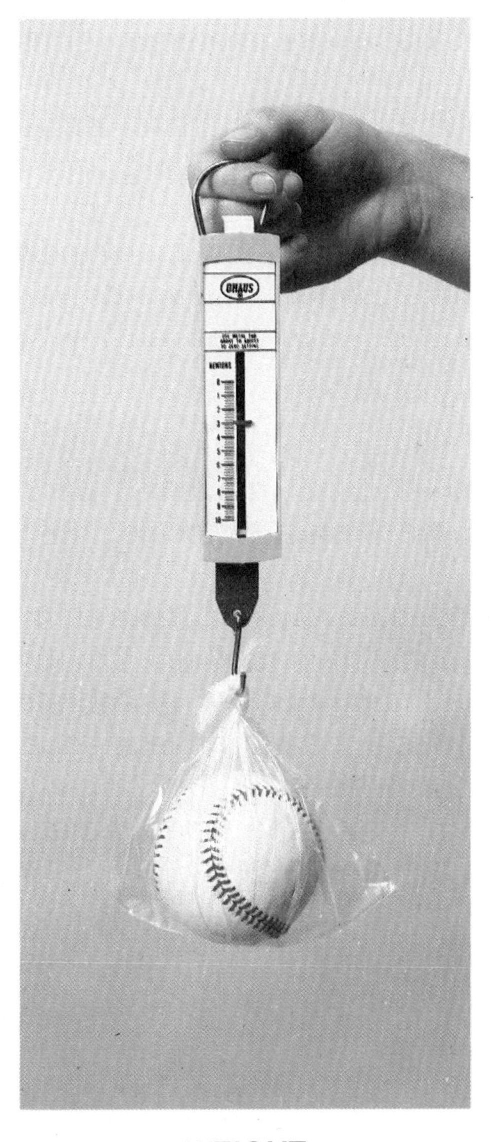

WEIGHT

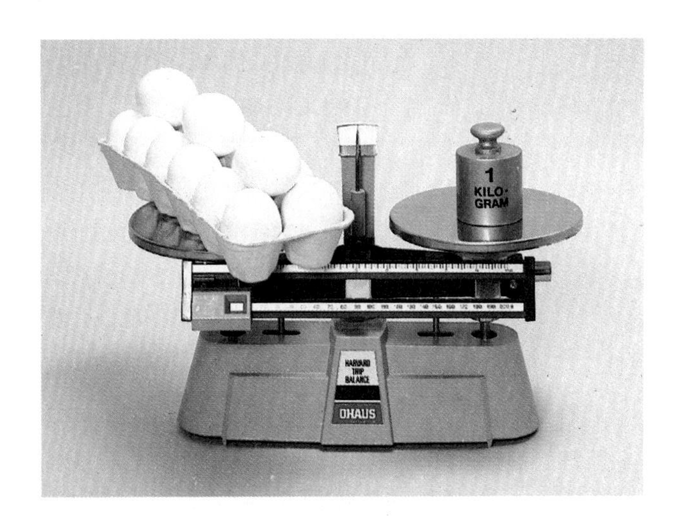

MASS

VOLUME

Index of Key Concept Terms: A Beginning Vocabulary For Science

In this index of key concept terms, you will find many of the words that scientists use. Scientists use many words that have a special meaning. You will want to use them correctly.

Some of these terms were new to you this year. Others may not have been, but all are important terms in science.

A page number is given for all of these terms. The page numbers tell you where to find more information about the terms.

As you study science, you will learn many new words and how to use them. Some of the words you already know may make the new ones easier to understand.

algae (AL·jee), simple green plants that do not have water tubes. Some grow on land. Most grow in water, 52

amphibian (am·FIB·ee·un), an animal that usually has two stages in its life. During the first stage it breathes in water. During the second it breathes air, 15

animal kingdom, the group of living things that are like animals in all important ways, 32

astronaut (AS·truh·naut), a person sent into space to study space and the bodies in it, 162

atoms (AT·umz), the small parts that make up a molecule, 188

backbone, a row of bones along the back of vertebrates, 20

bird, a warm blooded vertebrate that has feathers and lays eggs. Most birds can fly, 17

bison (BY·s'n), the North American buffalo, 227

calf, the young of a whale. Also the young of a cow, 220

carbon (KAHR·b'n), one kind of atom. It is a part of all living things, 188

cell (electric), a device that can store or release electric energy. A solar cell can change the energy of sunlight into electric energy. A dry cell changes stored chemical energy into electric energy, 97

chemical (KEM·ih·k'l) **change,** any change in a substance that changes the molecules. Burning is a chemical change, 192

chemical energy, a kind of energy that is released by chemical change, 97

chlorophyll (KLOR·uh·fil), a substance in plants that gives the leaves and stems a green color. It helps green plants make food, 34

class, a group of living things that are like one another in an important trait that is passed on from parent to offspring, 13

classify (KLAS·ih·fy), to group together things that are alike in an important way, 24

coal, a black or dark brown mineral, mostly carbon, which gives off heat when burned, 110

conserve (kon·SERV), to use wisely and keep from becoming used up, 78

coral (COR·ul), **animal,** an animal that has a soft body and lives in the sea. The coral is a hard material, like a skeleton, in which the animal lives, 222

coral reef, a stony barrier found around some islands. It is built of the hard materials made by coral animals, 222

decay (dee·KAY), rotting or breaking down of materials from plants and animals, 61

dissolve (di·ZOLV), to mix one substance into another so that you can no longer tell one from the other. Sugar dissolves in water, 180

dry cell, a device that changes chemical energy into electric energy, 97

electric energy, a kind of energy that flows through wires, 89

electromagnet (i·lek·tro·MAG·nit), a coil of wire around a metal bar. When electricity flows through the wire, the bar becomes a magnet, 99

energy (EN·er·jee), ability to do work, 87

environment (in·VY·run·ment), all things in and around the place where a plant or animal lives, 9

equator (i·KWAY·ter), a line that can be drawn around the Earth halfway between the North Pole and the South Pole, 138

evaporate (i·VAP·uh·rayt), to change from a liquid to a gas. Water evaporates and changes to water vapor, 173

evidence (EV·uh·dens), something to show that a statement is true, or that it is false, 145

fertilizer (FUR·t'l·y·zer), a substance used to improve the soil to make plants grow better, 77

fitness, what enables a plant or animal to live successfully in its environment, 204

flowering plants, a large group of green plants that have flowers and seeds. More new plants can grow from the seeds, 46

force (FOHRS), a push or a pull, 83

fossil (FOS·il), what is left of a plant or animal that lived long ago, 111

fuel (FYOO·el), anything that burns and gives heat energy. Coal and oil are fuels, 103

fungi (FUN·ji), a group of plants that do not have chlorophyll. They get their food from other living things, 41

gas, a form of matter. The molecules move freely about to take the shape of the entire container, 173

gill, a part of a fish that takes in oxygen dissolved in water, 14

humus (HYOO·mus), the decayed parts of plants and animals that have mixed with the soil. Humus helps plants grow, 61

jungle (JUNG·g'l), a very thick forest that grows in warm, moist parts of the Earth, with many animals as well as plants, 230

kingdom, living things are usually divided into two main kingdoms, the plant kingdom and the animal kingdom, 32

liquid (LIK·wid), one of the three main forms of a substance. A liquid pours and takes the shape of the container it occupies, 170

mammal (MAM·el), an animal that has a backbone and hair. Its young develops inside the mother, and is fed milk from the mother's body, 18

mineral (MIN·er·el), a substance, usually in soil or water, needed by living things. Minerals are needed in soil for plants to grow, 64

mixture (MIKS·chur), two or more substances blended together without changing the molecules, 182

model, an object that is used to explain the real thing, such as a globe as a model of the Earth, 188

mold (MOHLD), one of the kinds of fungi. Mold has no chlorophyll, 36

molecule (MOL·ih·kyool), the smallest part of a substance that acts like the substance, 177

mollusk (MOL·usk), an animal with a soft body and usually with a hard shell. Oysters and clams are mollusks, 25

moss (MAWS), a small green plant usually only a few inches high that can reproduce by spores. It does not have water tubes, 52

natural gas, a gas that is found underground with oil. It is used as a fuel, 115

nerve cord, the bundle of nerves inside a vertebrate's backbone. It connects all the nerves to the brain, 22

orbit (OR·bit), the path of a body in space as it travels around another body. The Earth is in an orbit around the Sun. The Moon is in an orbit around the Earth, 130

ovule (OH·vyool), the part within a plant's flower pistil that becomes a seed, 45

pest, a harmful or destructive animal or plant, 238

petal (PET·'l), a part of a flower like a leaf. It is usually colored, 43

petroleum (pet·ROH·lee·um), an oily liquid found underground. It is used as a fuel, and other fuels such as gasoline and kerosene are made from it, 114

physical (FIZ·ih·k'l) **change,** a change that takes place in a substance without changing the molecules, 192

pistil (PIS·til), the central part of a flower on which pollen must fall before seeds can form. The pistil holds the ovules, 44

planet (PLAN·it), one of several bodies in space that revolve around the Sun. The Earth is a planet, 129

plant kingdom, the group of living things that are like plants in all important ways, 32

pollen (POL·en), grains of yellowish powder formed on the stamen. It is needed for seeds to form, 44

pollen cone, the cone on pine trees that makes pollen, 46

pollinate (POL·ih·nayt), to transfer pollen from the stamen of a flower to the pistil, 45

pollute (pol·LOOT), to make something dirty or unclean, 195

radiometer (ray·dee·OM·ih·ter), a device that changes solar energy to energy of motion, 120

reproduce (ree·pruh·DOOS), to make more of the same kind, 5

reptile (REP·til), a cold blooded animal that breathes air and has scales or hard plates. It lays eggs with tough but soft shells. Snakes and turtles are reptiles, 16

root hairs, fine hairlike growths on the root of a plant. They take in water and minerals, 71

satellite (SAT·ih·lyt), a smaller body that revolves as a companion around another body in space. The Moon is the Earth's satellite, 124

seed cone, the cone of a pine tree in which seeds are produced, 46

solar (SOH·ler) **cell,** a device that changes solar energy to electric energy, 124

solar energy, any of the energy that comes from the Sun, 120

solar system, the Sun and all the bodies that revolve around the Sun, 131

solid (SOL·id), one of the three main forms of matter. A solid has a definite shape, 170

spore (SPOR), a special part of some kinds of plants that can grow into a new plant. Ferns, mushrooms, and molds have spores, 39

spore case, the part of some kinds of plants that holds the spores, 39

stamen (STAY·m'n), the part of a flower that produces the pollen, 44

stored energy, energy that is ready to be used, 89

substance (SUB·stuns), anything that takes up space and has weight, 178

theory (THEE·uh·ree), a reasonable explanation that seems to fit the facts or evidence, 116

vertebrate (VUR·tih·brit), an animal that has a backbone, 22

water vapor (VAY·per), molecules of water that move about separately as a gas. Water vapor is one of the gases in the air. It is invisible, 173

work, what is done when a force makes something move, 85

C 0 D 1 E 2 F 3 G 4 H 5 I 6 J 7